AF328559

Acquisition Syndrome

by

Dr. Tom Bibey

Acquisition Syndrome is a work of fiction. All the people and events in this novel are products of the author's imagination or used in a fictional manner.

Acquisition Syndrome
Copyright © 2012 Tom Bibey

All rights reserved. Including the right to reproduce this book in any form or portions thereof.

Designed by Rocio Almeida
Cover photography by Aldo Castellanos
Editor: Dorrie O'Brien

ISBN: 978-0-9827252-7-6

Library of Congress Subject Headings
Southern States - Fiction
Mystery - Fiction
Appalachia - Fiction
Bluegrass Music - Fiction
Medical - Fiction
Country Doctor - Fiction
Legal - Fiction

Dr. Bibey's amusing, yet authentic depiction of greed vs. good forced my attention in a single sitting. Acquisition Syndrome allows the reader to weigh the truths of today's fractured health care system through a country doctor's perspective and a cast of wich characters. The reader almost forgets it's just fiction! ----- *Kelly Jones*

In Acquisition Syndrome, Dr. Tom Bibey has moved from examining medical malpractice to the world of contemporary medicine practiced more in board rooms than in examining rooms as Bones Robertson seeks to protect his medical practice from the avaricious designs of the medical industry. Populated with his usual cast of bluegrass musicians, docs who want to practice humane medicine, golfers, and just plain folks, Acquisition Syndrome succeeds in exploring issues confronting medicine today in Dr. Bibey's gentle, folksy manner. A must read for readers of The Mandolin Case and followers of his blog. ------ *Ted Lehmann of Ted Lehmann's Bluegrass, Books and Brainstorms*

"There is something you can learn from every mandolin player you hear." ----- *Sam Bush, King of Newgrass and the right-hand rocking, reggae ruler of the Mandolin Universe*

"Dr. Bibey honors the truth and simplicity of rural southern life and traditional music. Finally, an author resists the hackneyed stereotype to accurately portray the integrity of bluegrass music and the people that love it." -----*Kristin Scott Benson, member of Grascals,   IBMA Banjo Player of Year 2008 and 2009*

"When a man writes like that, there has to be a reason."

Irene Lehmann

"We have known Dr. B for years. He is a good doctor,a serious amateur mandolinist, and a writer. Most of all…he is a man who cares about his people." ----- *Darin and Brooke Aldridge, the Bluegrass Sweethearts*

"I introduced Dr. B to bluegrass music and helped with his medical education. He has blended both of these disciplines into a metaphor for his story telling and view of life in general. My congrats on the publishing of his book. It will be well received." ----- *Dr. Peter Temple, Retired rural Family Physician and Community Medicine preceptor for East Carolina University School of Medicine*

"The visions you put in my mind, dance. A photo would squelch my dreams" ----- *-Billy Watson*

"Dr Bibey is Australia' s favourite American import. Who else combines country doctoring, mandolin picking and writing like he does? What a story, what characters, what a rip-roaring tale, Dr. B." ----- *Karen Collum, Australian Author*

Acquisition Syndrome

By

Tom Bibey

Ford, Falcon & McNeil Publishers
Chattanooga

I dedicate this book to my wife and children. They, along with my Faith, Family, Friends and Music, made my life. All the best to my readers, and thank you for reading my work.

Author's Note

Some of you may have read my first novel, *The Mandolin Case*, a medical malpractice mystery resolved by bluegrass pickers (with some help from golf-hustler Snookers Molesby).

My background is as a medical article writer, not a novelist, so I was very pleased with the success of my first book, selling around the world as it did. I attribute this to the uniqueness of the characters. I came to know them well, and they were so genuine I almost could not fail. With a cast like Dr. Henry ("Indie") Jenkins; Dr. Bones Robertson; Snookers Molesby; Mason Marley, a wise, blind, post-polio patient who lived on the river; Lucille Taggert, the lawyer for Physician's Liability, the big North Carolina malpractice carrier; Martin Taylor, a prominent plaintiff's attorney, and hosts of others, I didn't see how I could miss once people got to know them.

Many readers have asked what happened to Dr. James "Bones" Robertson after Indie died. The feedback was significant enough that I felt I should consider a follow up to *The Mandolin Case* with a sequel. I looked up Bones to see what he'd been doing since Indie's passing.

We met at the N.C. State Bluegrass Festival in Marion, N.C. one spring. Bones was now semi-retired due to an illness which had left him some physical impairment but it had no impact on his soul, spirit, or music. I found him in good spirits, and still enthusiastic about his role as a doc, even though he now served in an advisory role and no longer carried quite the same level of responsibility.

I soon found a lot had transpired in medicine that did not suit Bones Robertson. He was disappointed that medicine had undergone a gradual transformation. His biggest disappointment was that the practice of medicine had transitioned from a healing art to a business. After years of running a small business, Bones understood you had to make ends meet. "No tickee, no washee" and "No margin, no mission" were two of his catch phrases, but he believed patient care was not as personal after the big business approach took over the industry.

As in *The Mandolin Case*, Bones Robertson was a prolific note-taker. When we met in Marion he produced reams of paper that documented his thoughts regarding this transition. We discussed the possibility of transforming these notes into a novel. I agreed to take the notes home and study them.

That fall we met again at one of my book gigs, a fund-raiser at the Kinston Library. We also got together several times at Indie's cabin, which Indie had willed to Bones.

I again had my doubts as to whether I had the time or energy to transform all this material into a readable novel, but Bones was insistent. He believed this was a story that needed to be told and that I was the writer to do it. After months of organization by outlines, a year or so of writing, and then another half a year editing, the story finally began to gel into a readable story.

Acquisition Syndrome is the story of how Bones coped with changes in the medical industry in the last decade of his career. As in *The Mandolin Case*, the story is fiction, but shows the truth while it remains careful to tell no facts. All the names have been changed to protect the guilty, although if you lived in the area in those years you might recognize some of the characters. If you do, please don't give them up; if nothing else for your own safety—some of them have a vindictive side. We did decide to wait until Riley Harper's death to publish, though, and he was the one you had to watch the most.

One of the great joys of *The Mandolin Case* was all the new friends I made around the world. I hope you enjoy *Acquisition Syndrome* as much as my first novel. As always, I appreciate your feedback and look forward to hearing from you. I can be reached on my blog (see below) and I try to be responsive to my readers.

Visit my blog at http://drtombibey.wordpress.com or my website www.themandolincase.com

Chapter One

Dr. Bones Robertson finished hospital rounds on a fine Thursday morning in May and drove to the office. He parked his Chevy truck in the space marked The Doctor Is In, and checked his watch: 8:40 AM.

Won't have to rush today; on time for a change, he thought.

He sat down at his desk and began to sift through the lab reports and the mail.

Peg walked by. "Hey, Doc, how was your day off yesterday?"

"Great. Played the choose-up with the boys out at River Run. Snook was our 'A' man. I've never finished out of the money with Snook on my team."

"You really shouldn't gamble like that, Dr. Bones."

"Ah, Peg. It ain't like we play for any kind of high stakes. Everybody needs a vice."

"I suppose." She dropped the morning paper on his desk. "We just made some coffee. You want a cup?"

"Some of that from Ecuador?"

"Yes, sir."

"Sounds good. What's the news in the Harvey Herald?"

"Same ol', same ol'. Hey, did you know the Braves have won three in a row?"

"So I hear." Bones checked his watch. "Have I got fifteen minutes to look through the mail?"

"Yes, sir. Ezzie Watkins is first at nine."

"Cool. I hope she brings some of that pound cake. It's the best."

"It is that. Look at it this way: No matter how hard times get, your patients will never let you starve to death."

Bones smiled. "That's the truth." He opened a letter from one of the insurance companies. He read it, stared at it, put his feet up on the desk, twisted his moustache, and then twirled his stethoscope. "Man, I understand why Indie smoked. He predicted every bit of this. Is Dr. Dee here? I need to show this to him."

"Yes, sir. He's in his office."

"Thanks. I'll catch up with him in a minute."

By the mid-'90s, most of the primary care docs in Scotland Neck, North Carolina looked to Dr. Bones Robertson as the lead dog on the sled team. For a number of years, there was relative tranquility. Growth of the medical staff was slow, but Harvey County wasn't a hip new locale in *Southern Living*'s "places to live" list, either. Population growth was stagnant, but the people were older, so with the aging population the county needed a few more doctors.

Happily, every time the workload had become too heavy for the existing practices, the small but loyal band of local doctors would get lucky and find a new one.

Ed Dee had been one of those lucky finds. It wasn't every day when a med school professor set up shop in Harvey County, but Dee had grown bored with medical center politics and wanted to return to a rural life. He'd grown up on the farm, and enjoyed piddling on his tractor and liked to tend to his garden.

He and Dr. Bones Robertson, of Harvey Family Practice, hit it off right away. "Never saw anyone with as many initials after his name who wears Red Camel overalls," Bones said.

Dee was tall and redheaded. He had a wispy but full red beard with streaks of gray. He came up in rock 'n' roll and wore the little wire-rimmed glasses like John Lennon. He favored a Stratocaster guitar but also loved his D-35 Martin. Bones knew he had the right man when they negotiated their contract while they flat-picked "Soldier's Joy." They were done in an hour.

Years later, Dee ran across the contract in his desk drawer. It was all of three pages, and yet it covered the important ground. Dee showed it to his wife. "This thing is fifteen years old, yet we never amended it, and Bones held up to every promise."

Bones appreciated the compliment, but just shrugged his shoulders. "If all the docs want is a chance to take care of patients and be treated fairly there's nothing to a contract. The dang U.S. Constitution only runs twice as long. Here it is 1996 and that contract has held up for over two hundred and twenty years with very little amendment. It has to take into account the needs of a whole country; we're just one little doctor's office. We're smart; Jefferson was brilliant."

Local medical political dynamics had persisted with little change long after the Mandolin Case. Favor was not extended to the doctors with high Board scores or even the ones with the most robust practices. Instead, it tended to go to those who were willing to look the other way when the crew hired to pave the hospital parking lot re-paved the roads on the CEO's farm on the hospital tab. When the Harvey Hospital Board hired Marvin Stanley as the new CEO after Jim Olden left, Dr. Mike Blake met him at Raleigh Durham to drive him to his Harvey Hospital office. By the time Stanley had set up shop at the hospital, he and Blake were joined at the hip. Stanley declared that Blake was the "voice of wisdom" for the new CEO's strategy for health care delivery plans, which included consolidation of all the primary care practices under the Raleigh/CMA flagship.

Bones was not surprised, and said at the time to Dr. Ed Dee, "Dang fool new CEO hasn't known Blake for three hours, and he's already dubbed him as the 'progressive and wise voice of the medical staff.' Hell's fire, Blake never even passed his Boards. I know it for a fact. He's ABCDA: A Board Certified Dumb Ass, but that's the only certification he has."

Soon Blake was on the civic club tour as a medical spokesperson for Stanley's agenda.

"Already in Stanley's pocket," Bones sniffed.

Bones opened his mail one Monday and walked over to Ed's office. "Well, Dee. I guess my time's come to go."

"What do you mean?"

"Oh, it's just an old bluegrass tune. It's a gospel number but the title reminds me that we are gonna have to change the way we do the doc gig or end up driven out of business. Sort of like in your old music genre- Dylan would say "the times they are a changing."

"I agree with that," Ed responded.

"It's hard to be in the independent doctoring business anymore."

"Whatcha got there?" Ed asked.

"Look at this from the Blues." Bones tossed the paper on Ed's desk. Dr. Dee picked it up and peered at it over his Lennon glasses. Bones went on. "Our charge for a urinalysis is four bucks. The insurance company sent the patient a letter and said we had overcharged them by a dollar and a quarter. The patient was mad as all get out."

Dee took another look and lay the notice back on the desk. "You'd think people might not take the word of an outfit where the CEO makes six mil a year. We can't keep writing a buck and a quarter off all these tests and stay open."

"Well, they're gonna win the war of attrition."

Dee shook his head. "All that money is enough to give you the blues. Have you seen their office just outside of Durham?"

"Yeah, it's huge. Looks like a satellite movie set for Universal Studios. They can afford to ride it out. We can't. One heart attack for either of us and we can close the door."

"At least Lucas is young."

"Yeah, and she's better looking and smarter than us old geezers, too."

Harvey Family had been fortunate to find Dr. Janie Lucas, too. She'd joined the practice five years before Edward Dee came in. Lucas was more cosmopolitan than both of them put together. Her husband was a commercial pilot, and they loved to travel. But the farm had its appeal for her, too. Lucas raised Arabian horses. She'd bought an old cattle ranch out on Lee Highway, and she and her husband built a home and a horse barn on the property. She tended to her horses there when she was off.

"If the practice crashes, Lucas can afford to retire," Bones said. "She loves those horses. I can't say I blame her. If my spouse flew for U.S. Air, I'd want to be a gentleman farmer kind of doc, too. But we've been over-worked before, and I don't think she has any desire to do it again. I might have been able to a decade ago, but I don't have the stamina for the all-nighters anymore. Maybe you and I could go on a while, but I'm not so young anymore. I think the pace would wear us out."

"How's Billy doing?" Dr. Dee asked.

"He's fine. I'm still counting on him. There ain't a young person at Sandhills U. Medical Center other than Billy Spurgeon who'd even consider coming to Harvey County. If Billy hadn't grown up here and played golf for Harvey High, we'da never gotten him to take a look."

"Maybe if you hadn't promised him that old Scout of yours, he might've run away like the rest." Dee laughed. "What odds do you give us on him?"

Bones lit his pipe. "In the old days, I'd say a hundred percent. Billy is a good boy, and one of us. He wants to be a country doctor." Bones puffed away. "The question is 'Will society let him?'" Bones scratched his head and frowned. "Nowadays? Hm. I guess about fifty-fifty." Bones smiled. "You remember what Indie used to say after every argument at Medical Staff meetings?"

"Yes. It didn't matter what the problem was, the answer was always the same: 'Gentlemen, I don't know exactly what the problem is here but it has something to do with money.'

And he was always right. Our problem is we don't have the money or the power."

"So, how'd it go on the last recruitment trip?"

"You mean other than with Billy?"

"Yeah."

Bones sat down and propped his feet up on Dee's desk much like he'd seen Indie do years ago. He twirled his stethoscope for a minute. "When I talk to the young people there a couple times a year, I get some variation of the same speech every time. They say, 'Doc, I respect you. I appreciate when you took care of my aunt. You're one of the reasons I became a doc. But I know about what you make and exactly what you do every day, 'cause Billy and Gary and Julius and Richard have all been to Harvey County for community medicine rotations. I just can't do small-town private practice. I can make twenty-five percent more in salary at the walk-in clinic right out of school and never take a night of call.' And that's always the story."

"You never shoulda told 'em about the Scout." Dee laughed again.

"Hey, that old pony got me back and forth to the hospital a quarter million miles and I never got stranded; not even in the weather. She was a very reliable four-wheel hoss. I think if I'd been smart enough to get the four-point-three engine upgrade option at the time, she'd still be cantering." Bones twisted his moustache. "We all have our faults. She was just a bit underpowered, that's all; otherwise I'da held onto her. Got us to a lot of bluegrass gigs, too. Hated to trade in an old friend."

Dee pulled down his Martin off the wall and broke into the old Monroe number, "Goodbye, Ol' Pal." "Round about round up time in Texas way out west..."

Bones smiled. "Yeah, you're right. At least it wasn't a real horse. Coulda been worse. I'm just old-fashioned, I guess. Anyway, as far as the practice, I'm afraid we're like 'Gone With the Wind.'"

"I'm sure you're right. We've got a few years to work through it, though, but eventually we're gonna have to partner with someone bigger than us."

"The hospital has bought up a couple practices already."

"Maybe we better be like the Army."

"How's that?"

"We don't want to be first in line, but we don't want to be last, either."

Bones laughed out loud.

"Now that old CEO Olden is gone, maybe we have a chance for a fair deal," Ed said, hopefully.

"Yeah, but Marvin Stanley has the same judgment in doctors. They always scoop up the ones who can be influenced first. It's like Jimmy Stewart said in 'A Wonderful Life.' Potter wasn't selling; he was buying. It's nothing but a Monopoly game for these guys, but it's rigged. They have all the money."

"Discouraging."

"Yep. We'll just have to see how it plays out for us." Bones shook his head. "It would seem our interests have to be aligned with our hospital here, though."

"How interested are they?"

"Not very, as best I can tell. I talked to some of the Raleigh administration about a decade ago. They say they know they need a primary care base, but so far I haven't been able to interest them in any serious discussion. They had me talk to Olden back then and he was clueless about the daily operation of small practices. Maybe it's just that they know they can wait us out. The big boys have both the money and the time.

"I think the time has come for us to make the Raleigh boys get serious about making us an offer to join their organization. Why don't you go visit Stanley?"

"You want to go?"

"Nah. You go alone. Those CEO types always underestimate you."

"I guess it's the flannel shirts, or maybe it's the bluegrass picker in me."

"Maybe you oughta pick 'em a banjo tune."

"Yeah. How 'bout 'Don't Tread on Me'?"

"Brownie's tune?"

"Yeah, she's the one," Bones replied. "You know she moved to Raleigh not long ago to be near the grandparents? They have so much time on the road and it helps so much with their little boy. I managed to carve out the time to go up once a month for a mandolin lesson with her husband, John Wayne. The guy is a mando genius. They are a fine, true bluegrass couple. First Family of Bluegrass to me. You know, changing the subject here, I think I'll call Snookers Molesby. If there ever was a hospital insider he's the one. The guy is a scratch golfer so all the big shots call him to play on their team at the fund-raisers. Snook gets all the dirt and they don't know he's an informant."

Dee smiled. "Yeah, I know. Snook 'bout did in Jimmy Olden and the guy didn't know where he had a leak. When he left town, he paid Snookers to help him load up his things."

Bones laughed. "I hope the check didn't bounce."

Chapter Two

Bones set up a meeting with Stanley at the hospital for Thursday of the next week, and then called Snookers to see if he could play golf. He wanted to ask some questions about the hospital players.

They played nine holes on the following Wednesday morning, the day before the meeting with Stanley.
Snookers tallied up the card. "You've got a lot of game for a doctor."

"What's the damage, Snook?"

"Well, you get to pick up the tab at the Billiard and Bowl. I was one under, you're two over; we're slick, but I got it last time we broke even." Snook laughed. "You gotta admit, Doc, it's cheaper than lessons from the pro."

Harvey County was slow to change and the B-n-B was just the same as it was back in the days of The Mandolin Case with the same cheeseburger baskets and milkshakes. Lou still liked World Wide Wrestling on T.V. and always had popcorn and a PBR beer. One thing had changed; Harvey was no longer a dry county and you could now order a beer. You used to have to put an extra fifty cents in the Coke machine and press the Tab button for a PBR beer. Lou would get one for you if you were regular. One thing was the same. Lou enforced a strict two beer limit. "Ain't no one gonna run over no kid on Lou's watch."

When they arrived, Minnie the Myna Bird announced their presence with a loud whistle; a perfect imitation of an ambulance siren. Then she followed it up with a shrill chortle. "Bones is here. Bones is here!"

"When did that bird learn that, Lou?"

"She's gonna be able to announce all the regulars soon." Lou smiled. And if you hear Darth Vader's 'Imperial March' theme from 'Star Wars' you can count on the fact a stranger is in the house, and intuition says they might be no good. She's about got it down. You boys want your usual?"

"Yes, sir. And bring the bill to me. It's my turn to buy."

"Y'all played golf today?"

"Yes, sir."

"Lou, how about a beer?" Snook asked.

Bones waved his hand in approval. "Put it on my tab, Lou."

Lou left to get their order. Minnie let out a low wolf whistle, and Snook grinned.

"So, Snook, you still think Chick Crawley's a straight-up guy? Being a VP over at Harvey Hospital hasn't gone to his head?"

"Yeah, we play poker in Central Supply every Tuesday night. He never cheats. Still, he has to play the hospital political game to keep his job. He's better off not to know too much about any plans you might have to sell the practice yet. You can be sure if it doesn't work out, Marvin Stanley'd make him the fall guy in a heartbeat."

"I'm sure. Marvin better watch out, though. Chick has survived every administration 'bout since Hoover."

"That's the truth. If he was to be on that 'Survivor' show, the rest of 'em might as well go home."

"So, what do you know about this Riley Harper in Raleigh?"

"Not much. I can tell you who might, though."

"Who's that?"

"Bull Wilson."

"Bull? Is he still over at Phipsy's car lot?"

"Nope. His mama moved up from Baton Rouge. She's assistant manager at The Waffle House in Raleigh. Bull wanted to be near her, and got a job in Raleigh working for Simmons Rupert."

"Bluegrass Motors?"

"Yep. Bull heads up his pre-owned used car division. And Rupert is doing fine. He's one of the biggest dealers in Raleigh, both in new and used vehicles."

"I'm glad Bull's doing well; Rupert, too. How does Bull know Riley Harper?"

"Harper bought his mama an old Impala and—"

"An Impala? Nothing wrong with that, but good Lord, I heard the man drives a Porsche."

"Yeah, well, he tried to stiff Bull on the deal. Rupert had to threaten to take the SOB to small claims court, but he finally paid up. I think he was scared of Bull."

"Ah, Bull's a sweet boy, he wouldn't hurt anyone."

"Yeah, but they didn't let Harper know that. All he could see him for was his nickname. That neck of his is imposing. You know, 'Strong like Bull.'"

Bones laughed. "You're right. I'd be scared of him if I didn't know him."

Bones shook his head. "Sounds like I need to give Bull a call. It'd be good to see him anyway."

"Believe it would, Doc."

Chapter Three

As Bones drove into Raleigh he recalled the day Bull Wilson showed back up in Harvey County.

He hadn't seen Bull but a few times since Indie's funeral. He'd lived farther south for a while; somewhere around Tupelo. Rumor had it he'd gotten in a few scrapes with the law, mostly bar fights, usually something about a girl. When Bull came back home he went to work for Phipsy Motors, and later moved to Raleigh; something to do about a girl there, too, to start with, but he was all calmed down about the time he turned thirty, the testosterone poisoning had burned off and he'd begun to think a bit more clearly.

Bones slowed down. *Let's see, wasn't it the Waffle House on Hillsborough?* He checked the instructions Snookers wrote out. *Yep, this is the one.* He pulled in, went in, and scanned the waitresses' name tags. Adoette Wilson. *That's her.* "Ms. Wilson?"

She backed up a few steps. "Excuse me?"

Bones took his hat off. "It's me; Doc Bones Robertson."

"Why, Doc, Lord have mercy. I ain't seen you in years. How in the world are you? Bull just called; he'll be here in just a minute. What can I get you?"

"Two eggs, scrambled, pork chops. Coffee, high test."

She smiled and poured up a cup. "Bluegrass coffee: with caffeine."

In a minute Bull walked in. The boy was now a grown man with high cheekbones, jet black braided hair and eyes black as coal, a smile like a string of pearls, and a bull neck like an oak tree. He extended his hand. "Doc, how in the world are ya?"

"Fine, Bull, just fine. Had anything to eat?"

"Ain't nothing like Mama's home cooking at The Waffle House."

"I agree."

Ms. Wilson set a place for Bull. "Doc, Simmons Rupert says Bull is the best boy he ever hired."

"Awh, Mama . . . ."

"You still working on the banjo?" Bones asked.

"Yep. It's coming along. Brownie Scott moved to Raleigh. I was the first one to sign up for lessons."

"Man, a four-time IBMA champion. She could make a banjo player out of a doctor."

"She's good, Doc. Ain't no doubt."

Ms. Wilson brought Bull a plate of waffles. "Thanks, Mama." Bull poured on the syrup. "Snook said I might be able to help you."

"Might be. I'm looking for one of those CRVs for my daughter, Marie."

"Good bluegrass buggy. You know Mr. Rupert will cut you the best deal he can."

Bones laughed. "Yep. Simmons once told me to think of him like a sheep. He wanted me to shear him, he just didn't want me to skin him. I agree. He's gotta stay in business so he'll be there if I need a new car."

"That's Mr. Rupert, all right."

"Let me ask you something, Bull. You know a Riley Harper?"

Bull frowned. "Yes, sir."

"What do you think of him?"

Bull hesitated. Ms. Wilson poured up some more coffee then walked back to the grill. Bull lowered his voice. "Mama don't like for me talk bad 'bout nobody, Doc, but Mr. Harper ain't no good."

"How do you mean?"

"I sold him an old Impala for his mama. It was only five hundred bucks, and Mr. Rupert had to take Harper to small claims court to get the money. Shucks, the man drove a dadgum Porsche, and then to go and try to stiff Mr. Rupert such as that. Made me mad."

"Well, I don't like what I hear about the guy, but I'm afraid I'll have to deal with him." Bones finished off his eggs.

"You be careful, Doc. He trades like most white men did with the Native Americans."

"Thanks. I'll remember."

Chapter Four

Bones put on the morning coffee in the kitchen on the morning of his meeting with Stanley at the hospital. "Well, I guess the day is here."

Kate flipped some pancakes. "Oh, honey, you're still solvent."

"Yeah, at least we are this year. Might even be good for another couple of cycles." Bones tossed a few pancakes on a plate. "But my time's come to go. Big business has done gone and put an orchiectomy on us."

"It's such a shame."

"Yeah, it's curtains for the mom and pops, kiddo." Bones motioned a cut-throat sign across his neck and laughed. He poured up two cups of coffee, and handed one to her. "It is reality, though; it gets tighter every month. Dee and I talked it over. We figure we're one heart attack away from closing up shop. We've run the numbers. If either one of us is out of commission for six weeks, the expenses will overtake us. We can't even afford the overhead insurance anymore; too high."

"So, you're going to talk to Marvin Stanley today?"

"Yep."

"You sure you can do business with him?"

"I dunno. If Jim Olden were still CEO I'd say no, but I don't think this guy is that bad a weasel. We'll see." Bones sipped his coffee. "Hey, you remember when Olden was Santa Claus in the Christmas parade?"

Kate laughed. "Yeah. Whoever heard of Santa with a red beard? I don't remember how he got that gig, though."

"He had the hospital donate four hundred bucks to the new Volunteer Fire Hall. It wasn't anything but an investment to protect his half-mil job. Good grief. We haven't learned anything. Stanley's gonna be Grand Marshal this year. At least he won't be perched on that vintage red fire truck."

"I suppose his hair didn't match," Kate said.

"Yeah, I never saw a gray fire truck."

Kate tousled his hair. "Hate to tell ya, Doc, but I don't reckon you qualify, either."

Bones finished up breakfast, downed the last of his coffee, and put the plates in the sink. "Gotta go. I'll call ya."

She kissed him on the cheek. "Good luck."

Bones made rounds and made it to Stanley's office by nine. "Hey, Steph. Mr. Stanley in yet?"

"No, sir. He's usually late on Mondays. He called a little bit ago, though; should be here shortly. Have a seat."

"Okay, but I gotta be at the office in a half hour."

Stanley breezed in at ten after. "Come on in, James."

Bones stopped and looked behind him. "James? Who the heck is that? Since Indie nick-named me 'Bones,' no one calls me James except Mama, and she's earned the right."

Stanley shut the door behind them. "So, what's on your mind?"

Bones scratched his chin. "Hm. I guess about the same thing as everyone else. Survival."

"Yes. These are hard times."

"How's Bill Greene's practice going?"

Stanley cleared his throat. "Well, I think quite nicely, as far as I know."

"Don't you guys own it now?"

Stanley opened his desk drawer and shuffled around through some papers. "Now, James, Dr. Greene's business arrangements are confidential; you know that. What can I help you with?"

"Like I say: survival. I don't think it's any secret docs have a hard go these days, especially in primary care. I understand from 'Medical Economics' many hospitals have bought out practices these days to keep 'em from going under."

Stanley coughed. "We aren't in the subsidy business."

"Hm. Maybe you should look at it as an effort to salvage market share. One of these days other parties are gonna set up shop in town. When they do the gradual shift in referral patterns will amount to millions of dollars worth of business. I'd circle the wagons now before they get a foothold."

Stanley got up and walked toward the door. "Care for any coffee?"

"Sure, high test."

"Pardon?"

"You know, black with caffeine. Bluegrass coffee."

Stanley scrunched his eyebrows. "Hm. Okay." He opened the door. "Steph? Would you get us a couple coffees, please? One decaf and one, uh, high test." He came back in and sat down. "James, to be honest, we just aren't in the acquisition business. For one, it is not our area of expertise. Besides, the Feds frown on it; Stark Law, you know."

"Hm." Bones pretended to take notes, and began to doodle. Bones was but a large child, and bordered on ADD. Bored, he began to draw pictures of banjos the way he used to sketch on the church bulletin as a kid when the preacher got too long-winded.

Stanley shifted in his seat. "No, really. It is very unwieldy. In our market, we outsource all the practice acquisitions to—"

"Sandhills?" Bones laughed.

Stanley sputtered on his coffee a moment and set it down. "Not funny, James, not funny."

"Just kidding, Prez." Bones sketched out a flathead banjo on his note pad.

Stanley droned on. "Chevalier is still CEO over there at Sandhills. We're good friends, and have a good working relationship. Sixty-three percent of our cancer business goes to Sandhills U. Oncology, you know. He has no interest in disrupting a relationship that works."

Bones knew it was because one of the local oncologists went to med school at Sandhills and did his Continuing Medical Education updates there. He'd become interested in their oncology research. Administration did all they could to force his referral patterns to Raleigh but had not been able to break him free from his trust in consultants at Sandhills.

"I see."

Stanley got up and walked over to the window. "You know, I think it was terrible the way the medical staff turned on Jim Olden." He opened the curtain and looked at the Olden Cancer Center. "After all he did to build this organization."

"I don't know much about that." Bones sketched out a caricature of the old red-haired CEO. "So how's Blake's practice? Is he happy?"

"Blake? Oh yes, he's been very satisfied. You should call him. He says Capital Medical Acquisitions met all his needs. Blake says all he has to worry about is practicing medicine and he's glad to have the business burdens cast aside."

"Hm. Maybe I will. Hm. CMA, you reckon . . . . Uh, never mind."

"Really you should look into it, James. CMA is acquiring all the practices in our area, not only for us, but also a couple smaller hospitals in the nearby counties. I'd be glad to set up an appointment for them to talk to you and your partners. CMA is an excellent organization. I'm certain you'll be pleased. We do want to keep you in the medical family, you know."

Hm, Bones thought. *"That's what Olden used to say. Back in those days it meant "If you are willing to turn your head, we won't cause you any trouble; might even toss out a small reward bone every so often."* "Okay," he said. *Better send all your referrals to Raleigh, too,* he thought. "Whatever. We'll talk it over with 'em. But just to be clear, we are only in the exploration stage. I'm not sure what we're gonna do. We might stay independent."

"In good conscience, I have to advise against that. We believe everyone will have to align to make it. You can't go wrong with CMA. They are the experts in managing small practices so the doctors don't have to. Besides, they're all we have. We are too rural to attract anyone else."

Bones stuffed his note pad in his pocket. "I guess so. I'll talk it over with my guys. Give me a call."

"Will do, James. Good to see you."

Chapter Five

After hospital rounds, Bones thought he'd just pay another visit to Stanley's office. When he asked Stanley's assistant, Stephanie, if the man could see him again, she told him Stanley had just left for a meeting.

Bones stopped at the desk, leaned over, picked up the newspaper, and flipped through it. "Hey, ya'll 'bout keep the Harvey Herald in the ad business all by your lonesome."

"Have a seat, Dr. Bones," she said.

He sat down. "Hey, Steph, how's the boss?"

"Okay, I guess."

"You're a reliable girl. You keep secrets okay?"

"Yes, sir."

"This new guy got Olden's disease?"

She got up and checked around the corner, and walked back to where Bones sat. "Well, maybe not as bad, sir. At least he doesn't chase women."

"So what's his Achilles heel?"

"Uh, well . . . I don't . . . I mean . . . ."

"Look, Steph, I ain't gonna tell. You gotta keep your job. If I caused you any trouble every beauty operator in town would make my life hard."

She smiled. "Well, he's a political sort. Always says he serves at the pleasure of the Board. And nowadays that extends to Raleigh; that CMA crowd runs it all ever since they got the lease on Harvey Memorial."

"How are they to deal with?"

"Oh, they come in here and complain how country we are. You can't please 'em. One day we had Mrs. Brackett's homemade red velvet cake for dessert and one of those fancy fools said they preferred store-bought."

"Dang, that is bad judgment. If they turn it down again, send it to me."

"Yes, sir. Want a cup of coffee?"

"Sure."

"I assume your usual. Bluegrass, high test, no cream, no sugar."

"Correct. So I take it Stanley's not gonna make any big decisions as to how to align with the docs without CMA's blessings? His job depends on it."

She set the coffee down. "Matter of fact, he said that very thing to his wife yesterday. Heard it myself. He's gonna do what it takes to make them happy."

"Tell me what you know about this Stark law."

"They talk about it all the time, but I've never seen it in print. My understanding is that it is more a complex set of regulations no one knows how to interpret."

Bones scratched his head. "That's the way I see it, too, but I am certain the Feds regulate how much hospitals are allowed to pay for a practice. The rules regulate the buy-outs these days. And any contractual arrangement that offers incentive for referrals is strictly forbidden, as it should be.

Where the patient is referred to should always be based on their choice."

"That's why the patients like you, Doc. And I agree with you. I understand even CMA knows to avoid that minefield."

"Speaking of CMA, I'm not sure it's so good to have no local control of our policies. Take the EMTALA patient transfer laws, for example. Administration doesn't like it if we don't refer to Raleigh and yet if you can't get anyone to accept a transfer of a patient, it can be trouble. This is a fine hospital and can do a lot of good things, but you don't need to advertise you're more than what you are. If you get a patient admitted here who should have been admitted to a bigger facility, well, try getting an emergency transfer on the weekend and you'd see what I mean."

"Really? Has it ever happened?"

"I saw it happen in Croatan County one time. The Bonfield case way back in the early 'eighties. I used to sit on the NC Malpractice Review Board and I heard a lot I can never tell. I will tell you this, though: When trouble showed up not a single one of the coat-and-tie guys offered a bit of support. None of 'em came to the doctors' defense. One of the docs had zero legal exposure and did all he could to protect the hospital's interest and still tell the truth. They still tried to ruin him. It was ugly. Heck, they even sent some beady-eyed little lawyer fellow to try to bury the docs, but he failed miserably. Didn't know a fart from a heart attack. The jury knew he was just after money."

"Tell me more."

"I've said too much already." Bones sipped his coffee. "All confidential. Besides that, it'd take a novel to tell the whole story. Anyway, going back to Stanley, to some degree I do understand why he's in the spot he's in. All those guys survive on political favor and not much else. We all do to some degree, I guess. In your job, you gotta do what you have to do to make him happy. Well, only up to a point, of course."

She laughed out loud. "Yes, sir, I understand. He's never acted wrong toward me, though. If he did, Roger'd kick his ass."

"I'm sure he would. Tough boy." Bones finished his coffee, crumpled up the styrofoam cup and tossed it in the trashcan. "You think Doc Bill Greene is happy the way his practice was set up?"

"Pretty much. Not all perfect, but okay. He comes around to complain some, but I think it has worked out okay. Melanie, one of his secretaries, has been with him since he started the practice. She says he's doing okay and finds it better to be part of the big organization than having to go it alone."

Hm, Bones thought, Snook said the same. "So is Roger still racing motorcycles?"

"Yes, sir."

"Tell him Bones said to be careful."

"I will."

Chapter Six

After his afternoon meeting, Marvin Stanley checked in with Chick Crawley. Chick had started working at Harvey Memorial in high school in Central Supply for a summer job. He got on in administration right out of college and had been there ever since, working his way up through the ranks. He made VP after Jim Olden left, not so much on the basis of his education, even though he had a four-year degree. It was more because it was about even odds the hospital operation would grind to a halt without him.

Chick was one of the last walk-ons on the UNC basketball team and played one season for Dean Smith. He still walked with more spring than most men decades younger, and kept his hair the same consistent sandy blond, though he let a little gray creep in at the temples after age fifty. Chick knew every secretary, and all the custodians. He sent a card to each nurse on their birthday, played golf with the docs, and went to Rotary Club and Harvey First Methodist with all the Board members. He'd modernized the hospital's billing system and hobnobbed in Raleigh with State Senator Rich Walton. Rumor had it Walton wanted Chick to be his campaign manager when he ran for Lieutenant Governor. In a word, Chick was connected.

"So, can we get Bones under the CMA umbrella?" Stanley asked Chick.

"Probably."

"Probably? What choice does he have? No one's gonna come here to compete with us."

"I don't know, boss." Chick got up, opened the blinds, and stared out the window. "Don't forget Sandhills. They sure did sniff around Bill Greene's practice."

"Yes, but he's in Croatan County, an hour east of here. I don't believe Sandhills will come this far. Not enough market share for the investment and not enough referrals to warrant it. Raleigh has it locked up."

"Sandhills can't expand any farther east. They already have the Outer Banks and there aren't too many practices out in the Atlantic Ocean. I wouldn't count them out for going west."

"Maybe." Stanley got up, walked to the window, and pointed down the street. "Did you secure the property down by Eckerds?"

"Nope. The Board didn't approve it."

"The Board, the Board. They just think they run this place. The brains, and the power, that's at CMA in Raleigh. Don't forget it. We need to can that car dealer Rick Lester. We don't need his kind on our Board. He's not worth a damn on it; he just uses us for information. You know that lot I had my eye on for the new Radiology Center? SOB scooped me on it for a damn car lot. He's up for re-election next month. Get him off the Board."

Chick shook his head. "Boss, I'd be careful not to piss Lester off. You know who his competition is?"

"What do I care?"

"Phipsy, boss. Phipsy."

"Who's that?"

"Good Lord, boss, he's one of those bluegrass people. 'Phipsy's Honest Used Cars, only the best for the best.' He plays bass. He's friends with that entire Bones Robertson crowd. You better keep Lester on your side. He's the only car dealer you've got."

"Hm. He only wants the property so if any competition ever came to town they'd have to buy it from him. I could see Sandhills putting an office there where I'd have to look at it every day. It wouldn't have to make any strategic sense; Chevalier would enjoy the pissing contest."

"I could be wrong on them coming this far west, of course. So far they don't plan on it, though."

"How sure are you?"

"Not positive, but it seems unlikely. Snookers dates one of the secretaries at Chevalier's office."

"Snookers?"

"Snookers Molesby."

"Who's that?"

"Central Supply. I play poker with him down there on Tuesdays."

"Damn, Chick. I don't pay you to play cards."

"Whatever, boss. Maybe you should, though."

"What does he do here?"

"He's head of maintenance."

"Hm." Stanley's cell flashed a message and he checked it.

"So," Chick asked, "does Riley Harper still buy all the practices for CMA?"

"Yes. Riley Harper. He's a good man. He's been in charge of all the practice acquisitions for Capital Medical Acquisitions for the better part of a decade, and man, has he cut some deals. If we had stockholders, he'd be very popular with them. Riley has made it clear: We can't have another Greene fiasco. Harvey Memorial owns fifty-one percent of it and CMA manages it, but he says it's too hard to control and he won't do it again."

"Greene? Hard to manage? He's a good doc."

Stanley shook his head. "SOB drives me crazy with all these notions about quality health care delivery systems. Screw that. He should have wound up in Raleigh's camp a hundred percent. Riley coulda dealt with all that but it ended up as my problem since Harvey Memorial owns a majority share of the practice. Greene calls me every Tuesday with some kinda question about patient care. I don't have time to deal with all that. I don't want to ever own any part of another practice; let CMA have it all."

Chick thought back on the hybrid deal they'd cut with Greene: The hospital had majority share, but CMA managed it, and Greene thought the hospital ought to help him run his practice the way it needed to be run. "Well, Bones is an idealist too, better watch out. He won't be satisfied to have too little control over what he can do for his patients, and Raleigh isn't gonna give him an inch. It's their way or the highway. Riley Harper isn't a physician and has no compassion, either. I doubt he and Bones would get along very well."

"Bones is a damn Don Quixote. We don't have the capital and I don't have the time for dreamers who chase windmills. Just make sure Bones doesn't defect to Sandhills. I don't think they'll come this far west, but it would be trouble if they did. Raleigh has our lease, they want our patients, and I want my job."

"I suppose, boss, but I gotta tell you, one of these days if we don't partner with these docs directly, the alliance is gonna fracture."

"What do you think the odds are Sandhills will talk to Bones?"

Chick rubbed his chin. "I don't think they'll come this far west. For them to do it, they'd have to have a player on the inside. Bones Robertson is a loyal sort. I don't think he'll leave. But I do think they'll talk to him if we are dumb enough to leave the front door unlocked and let 'em walk in the house."

"Then don't let it happen." Stanley sat down at Chick's desk and drew out a map. "Yeah, Greene's in Croatan County. We had to protect Greene's practice. I still think we did the right thing. It's a damn fertile crescent for referrals, and they coulda gone either way. I play enough golf with Chevalier to get a read on him. I don't think he'll drift this far. It's just too far for any significant exodus of referrals. Plus, he doesn't want to pick a fight with me since we have CMA on our side; we've got too much power for them to overwhelm us. Bones has no leverage."

"I suppose, but I'd still be careful."

"Damn it, Chick. This should be an easy one. Get Bones delivered to Raleigh. My job depends on it and yours depends on me."

"Yes, sir, boss. Yes, sir. It shouldn't be a problem."

Stanley called Bones. "I've talked this over with Mr. Harper. He's more than willing to meet with you."

"I'm sure."

"Wednesday lunch okay?"

"I'll check with my partners, but I think so."

"Wonderful. Let me know. You'll love Riley Harper. Top-notch man."

"Like family?"

"Exactly." Stanley hung up the phone and called out to his secretary. "Stephanie, a coffee, please, and for God's sake, don't ask me about that damn bluegrass coffee."

"Yes, sir."

Chapter Seven

By the time Bones Robertson was sneaking up on retirement age, he had his heart set on a young man named Billy Spurgeon being the doctor who might help him at Harvey Family Practice and carry it on after Bones retired. He knew there weren't many left in the community like Billy Spurgeon: If there was any human being on the planet who might come back home to Harvey County, instead of deserting it for the big city and big money, it was Billy.

Bones was up front about it, too. When Billy would come home to visit, Bones would tell him, "Billy, I sure hope you come home. We need help big time."

And Billy would reply the same way every time: "Like I promised, Doc, I'll always take care of you."

Billy was as homegrown as an ear of Silver Queen corn; a kid whose idea of a night on the town was to take his girl to the Magnolia Restaurant at the Holiday Inn in Scotland Neck or "The Plantation" over in Maxton, and then go out to the picture show. His dad taught math at Harvey County High School and raised tobacco and cattle on a small farm, so Billy was used to real work. He'd gone to Harvey County High, played trumpet in the band, and was third man on the golf team. In fact, Bones served as an assistant coach during those years, though his schedule as a doctor precluded any regular attendance at practice. One time Bones told Billy his only regret was he didn't finish his Eagle Scout as a kid. When Billy made Eagle, Bones was the first person to call and congratulate him.

Billy was tall, lanky, and had jet-black hair. He was somewhat myopic, with the introspection that often comes along with spectacles. As a kid he wore black-rimmed glasses, but as he got deeper into bluegrass he switched to tortoise shell horn-rims and never changed styles after that. Other than an adequate hand/eye co-ordination that allowed for a decent golf swing and an above-average ping-pong game, he was only an average athlete. Too slender and not aggressive enough for football, too slow afoot for track, not enough vertical leap to do much with basketball, like Bones, he knew his future was in books.

He first met Bones Robertson as a high school student in the Medical Explorers' Club. After a meeting, Billy wanted to know more. Bones and Ed Dee invited him out to eat at Chang's Chinese.

Even years later, Dr. Ed Dee laughed about it. "Bones about ran the kid off before we ever had a chance. After lunch, when the boy was ready to go home, Bones walked him by that old Scout of his. Lord, he drove the thing to a quarter million miles. Bones would slap that Scout on the rear fender and his hand would turn pink from the oxidation of that old red paint. 'Now, son,' Bones said. 'You have a chance to be just like us. If you work hard and you're honest for a lifetime, all this can be yours.' A wonder the boy didn't leave right then."

Bones always said every student he did that with had gone into a subspecialty in the city. When it didn't scare Billy off, all three docs at Harvey Family knew they had a young man who might just go the distance.

When Billy interviewed for med school, they asked him why he wanted to be doctor. He said, "I'm a lot like Dr. Bones Robertson. I'm good with books, and I want to help people."

"That's what they all say," they said.

As it turned out, it was true.

Billy and Bones stayed in touch all through medical school, and Billy did a couple community medicine rotations at Harvey Family Practice. Billy said his best prep for Boards was over lunch at Chang's Chinese, where Bones took him out to eat every Friday on the "Starving Medical Student Foundation" fund. Bones seldom forgot a case, and the two spent the lunch hour poring over everything from hemachromatosis to celiac sprue to Whipple's disease. It would have bored any normal human being, but Billy soaked it all up, took notes, and then went home and read *Harrison's Text of Medicine* on the subject.

He was a good student. He made the seventy-fifth percentile on Part I of the Boards, an excellent score. But Billy had one quality that made him a standout potential recruit at Sandhills U. Medical School: He wanted to come home and practice medicine in Harvey County. He was the only one.

Bones called Billy after Labor Day, six weeks after Part Two of the Boards, and right before Billy started residency. "Hey, kid, how'd Part Two of the Boards go?"

"Okay, Doc. No problem. I just answered the questions the way I thought you would."

"You're a good young'un. How'd ya do?"

"Ninety-second."

His ninety-second percentile was the third best score in the class.

"Doc," he told Bones, "I did just like you. I didn't forget the patients, and I knew I'd read the answers somewhere. Then all I had to do was fill in the right bubbles. No sweat."

"Yep. Sounds like me. Couldn't quite get to the top of the mountain, but got close."

"I'll climb the hill with you anytime, Doc."

Bones always said Billy was the new and improved version of himself. "Yep, that was my strategy, kid. I never forgot the people; they led me to the answers. Of course, the docs at the top of the intellectual heap can recall what page and the exact journal article where they read it. I wasn't that good."

"Yeah; but if they don't put the patients first that wouldn't be any kind of country doctor, would it?" Billy asked.

Bones smiled. "I guess not. I'm gonna be down after flu season. Me and Kate like to go to the beach before it gets quite so crowded. Can I drop by?"

"Sure."

Billy stayed at Sandhills for residency. True to his word, he stuck with primary care, and wanted to talk to Bones about coming back home. They met at the med student library. "You know, Doc, I think it is so cool they named this thing after you."

"Uh, Billy, it was really named after my dad. He gave most of the money."

"Maybe so, but when we think of the Robertson Library, we think of you."

"That's 'cause when you play the mandolin, it is such a public thing you get more attention than you deserve, but I do appreciate it. I gotta admit, Dad had a great idea and I did contribute. If you think about it, it is kind of appropriate. Without books I'd've never made my way. I never was a tough guy."

"You are when you have to be, and you are in your own way," Billy said.

"Maybe so."

Billy picked up a copy of *Medical Economics* off the table. "I read this thing every month. They say it is hard times for small practices. You guys still okay?"

"We're in survival mode, Billy, but we can still pay the bills. The magazine is right, though. By the time you get very far into practice, I think most small practices will have to align with larger organizations to survive, ours included."

"No surprise," Billy said. "None of our guys plan to enter private practice, much less start one from scratch. What move do you think you'll make?"

"Too early to say. Just in the beginning of the talking stages right now. These things always move slow, pal. It's hard for docs because we have to make decisions in a hurry or someone dies. I get bored when people piddle over minutia." Bones paused to think. "I hate to tell ya, but the rest of your life you're gonna have to fight to be a family doctor or a general practitioner; the biz guys rule nowadays. My bet is the battle will boil down to Riley Harper at CMA out of Raleigh, versus Sandhills, at least if we can interest the University in our neck of the woods. My loyalty is still with Harvey Memorial and will be unless they are unreasonable, but I gotta admit part of my heart is still at Sandhills because I went to school there. Anyway, all three of us docs at Harvey Family will have to be careful what we do. We've run a small business for years but we are Big-Biz-Shark neophytes and we're gonna need help to survive the changes coming, not only in government but also the insurance world."

"I'm sure you'll figure out some way to make it all work."

"As soon as I do, I'll let you know. I know I can still offer the salary I've promised. It could be a bit more; I just don't know yet."

"It's okay. I want to come home and work here. I know you'll do the best you can. I trust you."

"Tell you what, son. It's okay to trust me, but I might drop over dead next week. As best I can tell, you better not trust too many people in the doc biz. How much debt do you have?"

"About a hundred grand. Not too bad compared to most of my classmates."

"Hm. You might be able to afford to be a family doc. You got out pretty light."

"Yeah, the old Indie Jenkins/Betty Wilson scholarship saved my butt. You knew him pretty good, didn't ya?"

Bones smiled. "Yeah, sure did." *Indie would be proud.*

In Billy's last year of his Family Practice residency, Bones brought him a sample contract to work at Harvey Family Practice much like the one he and Ed Dee had signed together, years ago. Billy and Bones went over the contract in a picking session at Robertson Library.

The librarian ran them off before they finished. "Now, gentlemen, this is too much noise, you'll have to move outside."

"Yes, ma'am." Bones gathered up the contract. "Hey, you gotta admit, though, at least its good music."

She smiled. "I suppose. With a little polish you could put on a show."

Bones laughed. "We could have gotten someone who knew what they were doing to polish us up and put on a show, but we were afraid someone would think we played country music."

She scrunched her eyebrows. "Is what you play not country music?"

"No, ma'am, it's bluegrass."

She scratched her head.

Bones said, "Oh, don't worry, ma'am. You're right. It's the true country music."

She motioned them toward the door. "Now, boys, you must move on. Bones, you tell your mother I said hello."

"Yes, ma'am. She'll be glad I'm still hanging out in libraries."

"She was a wonderful English teacher."

"Yes, ma'am."

They moved negotiations over to the Croatan Grill and set up on one of the picnic tables out front. "Old lady

Wilkins likes the music more than she lets on," Bones said. "Did you see her foot? I think it was tapping just a little bit."

Billy laughed. "Yeah, but she wasn't gonna get carried away with it."

The wind blew one of the contract pages across the parking lot. Bones retrieved it and sat back down. "You know Billy, you could do a lot worse than to stay in North Carolina. Here it is March and we're outside in shirtsleeves."

"I don't want to go far, Doc. I'm a homebody, you know that."

Bones got out his mandolin and rendered a few bars of "Carolina on My Mind." "I'm a homebody, too, but you need to be sure. These days anyone in primary care is gonna get big city offers from all over."

"I know, but I want to stay here at home."

"You sure? Small town life is great for me, but it has its own set of pressures. You have to accept you'll be under the microscope all your life. If I go to the grocery store, folks look in my cart to see if I'm eating what I recommend to them."

"I'm sure."

"And Angie?"

"She's okay, too. We've talked it all over."

Bones picked up the contract. "Okay. Now look here at page three. This thing is pretty simple, but I want to be sure you understand it."

"Sure." Billy read it over. "Don't you have a non-compete clause?"

"That's the industry standard these days, but we are different at Harvey Family. I came up with ours myself."

Bones pointed out the line. "Ours is called a 'right to compete clause.'"

"What does that mean?"

"As bad as our practice needs you, Harvey County needs you even worse. You won't be a full partner for a year, but if for some reason it doesn't work out, we want you to stay in town. This clause means if you leave our practice and stay in Harvey County you have to agree to share call with us when you go out on your own. We're tired. We need the coverage a whole lot more than we need to screw you out of a few bucks. And the county needs to hold onto all the good young people we can." Bones got out his pipe. "You mind if I smoke since we're outside?"

"Nah, it's okay."

"If Indie were alive he'd fuss," Bones said. "He was flattered I took after him, but he made me promise never to take up cigarettes. He hoped I'd never get started but the older I get the more I understand the pressure he was under . . . . Oh, well, at least it's not cigarettes and only once a week or so . . . . I can understand better now." Bones looked over the contract again. "You know, Billy, this all should be so simple. You wouldn't believe what kinda contracts all the biz guys come up with. You 'bout gotta give away your first born child if you leave. Dang . . . ." Bones lit his Granger's and took a puff. "By the way, let's ink in a potential start date."

"I finish residency end of July this year. I think I could be ready to go in two weeks."

"We'd love to have you as soon as you can start, Billy, but I'd recommend a full month off and start in August. That way you'd make partner by late summer of '97."

"Any significance to the date?" Billy asked.

Bones took another puff on his pipe. "Not really. But I do think you'd be better off to already be a partner before we make any final decisions about alignment with bigger organizations. Harder for them to mistreat you if that is the case. At the pace that process is going our simple business relationship should beat that time-line easy. I figure it'll be late '97 and probably mid '98 before we see any acquisition plans gel. So, a month one way or another doesn't matter. I'd like to see you take some time off with Angie before you jump in the fray anyway. I promise you Billy, private practice is the official end of summer vacation for a young man. You'll find you can't take much time off in primary care and stay afloat."

"So what's the downside if I should leave the practice?" Billy asked.

"It costs some to recruit and take a chance on you, even though you aren't exactly a flight risk. And it'd cost money to find someone to replace you, too, though the truth is not many are gonna come along who want the job. Any profit you make over and above your base salary, you'd have to leave behind. Don't worry, it ain't gonna be much. You could still afford to set up your own shop, if that's what you wanted to do."

"I doubt I'd want to. In fact, no one in my class plans to."

"I can't blame 'em. I wouldn't want to start one nowadays. There're too many regulations written by too many people who make too much money and don't know a dang thing about sick people." Bones puffed away. "And they sure don't care nothing about 'em." He frowned. "Anyway, we hope you want to stay with us a long time."

"I'm sure I will." Billy looked over the contract one last time.

"Did you get a lawyer to look it over like I told you?" Bones asked.

"Yes. He said it was fair, but it sure was simple."

"You know what my daughter says . . . ."

Billy laughed. "Yeah, Doc. You're so simple you're complicated to people."

"You can take it back to him if you want to."

"Nah, I think he'd just make it too confusing."

They shook hands and Billy and Bones both signed at the end on page four. "You want to go to the Dixie Queen for supper?" Bones asked. "I could stand some of that flounder."

"Sure."

Bones slapped him on the knee. "Let's go; it's still on the 'Starving Medical Student Foundation' tab."

On the drive home after dinner, Bones thought back to a boy named Walter Quigley from a few years back. Walter's daddy had owned a string of corporate eastern North Carolina pig farms. Walt was a bright student and had made excellent marks at North Carolina State.

His dad had come by to ask Bones a few questions. "What kind of money can the boy expect to make as a doctor?" he'd asked.

Bones handed him the latest *Medical Economics* survey on primary care salaries. Bones explained, "Some of those numbers are a bit optimistic, especially for the ones still hanging on in private practice. The rate controls from big insurance and big government, plus the increased overhead from the documentation requirements have taken a toll. Imagine if you had to fax me to get approval for your every move in the pig biz. I don't know a thing about pig farming and most of the people I have to get on the phone with are equally uninformed about doctoring. All it would do is slow you down and make you less efficient."

Mr. Quigley looked over the numbers again. "Good Lord, the boy could do that well with Oink, Inc., right out of college. Why should he bother?"

Bones' second partner at Harvey Family Practice, Janie Lucas, was in the grocery store the next week and overheard a group of ladies talking about young Quigley. One said, "I hear Walter Junior is going to be a doctor. Isn't that wonderful?"

"I suppose," Mrs. Quigley answered, "but there sure isn't any money in it."

Walter finished medical school, but never considered primary care. He went on to law school, too, and then became a mid-level insurance executive for one of the conglomerates. He started out at three hundred grand a year, more than twice what a country doc like Bones could earn for an around-the-clock routine that had gone on for years.

No wonder it was hard to get young people in the biz. Even their mamas were against it.

Chapter Eight

Robertson, Dee, and Lucas met for a pre-CMA conference discussion. Bones opened the meeting. "Such a shame it came to this, but I don't see how we can go on without some big changes, guys."

Lucas set down her pencil. "Not your fault, B. Greene's already out. Blake sold out to Raleigh a long time ago. There's a reason not many independents are left."

They shuffled through the financial statements. Bones laughed. "I don't see how we can do the fishes and loaves routine much longer."

"Damn Blues have 'bout strangled us to death," Lucas added.

"Did you see that commercial they had on TV? Some little girl got hurt at the lake and the insurance company brags they *let* her go to the best doctors? Dang hypocrites. That commercial costs more than our annual budget. Where do they get off deciding who *gets* to go where? What if they don't like you? Do they make you go to the bad doctors?"

"Better watch out, Bones." Dee laughed. "I doubt they like you very much."

"Probably not." Bones shook his head.

"We don't have a choice," Lucas said. "We have to consider all our options. Have you told Billy Spurgeon about all this?"

"I've kept him in the loop. He understands. Billy is just like all the residents these days, they'd rather just get a job and work for someone than try private practice. The only reason he's signed with us is because it is us. I'm sure deep down inside he hopes we'll eventually join forces with some larger entity. These days it is a matter of security for the future, especially for the young doctors. We all gotta align somewhere and right now the Harvey Memorial and CMA alliance are the only two games in town."

"I agree," Dee said. "Let's go see what the Raleigh boys have to say. We don't really have a choice but to explore our options."

Bones studied his notes. "I tested the water about ten years ago, guys, and it wasn't pretty. At that time, the attitude was we could take it or leave it."

Dee laughed. "You know what? Those guys couldn't diagnose sepsis if it slapped them in the face. How'd they wind up owning all this?"

"Pretty simple," Bones said. "They spend all day every day angling for power, control, and money. We spend all our time trying to figure out what to do for a bunch a sick people. We all do what we do, and we aren't business guys."

Lucas scratched her head. "No surprise we all got outmaneuvered."

"Well, let's go," Bones said. "I don't know a thing about business, but let's look at this like a car deal."

"How's that?" Lucas asked.

"If they make an offer, tell 'em you gotta talk to your husband."

"That shouldn't be hard. Everybody thinks we're married anyway. Speaking of car deals, how's Phipsy these days?"

"Good. I talked to him last week. He advised I check in with Simmons Rupert in Raleigh."

"Bluegrass Motors?" Ed Dee asked.

"Yep. Bull Wilson went to work for him up there."

"Oh, good." Lucas smiled and tapped her pencil on the desk. "Bull is such a sweet boy."

'Yeah, 'cept for that neck on him," Bones said. "I believe I'll check in with Simmons Rupert before the meeting with Harper." Bones handed them a card with Harper's contact information. "Meet me there at three-thirty."

Bones stuck his head in the restaurant and spotted Simmons from across the room; he recognized his straw hat that hung on the post by the booth before he even saw Rupert. Simmons Rupert was a slender, hyperactive man whose already quick speech was pressured after many years at the Capitol City car auction. Like Bones, his survival depended on accurate assessments of situations, often under time pressure. Bones approached the table and Simmons stood up to shake hands.

"How's the banjo world, Simmons?"

"Great. We've got Brownie Scott in for a show next month. Y'all oughta come."

"Probably will. She's a player." Bones checked out the menu. "How's the catfish sandwich?"

"Excellent."

The waitress took their order. "One check, please," Bones said. "It's my turn to buy." In a minute she brought their plates. Bones munched on his sandwich. "Lord, I love good salt-and-pepper cats."

"Big Ed's at City Market is the best, no doubt."

"Tell me what you know about Riley Harper," Bones asked.

Simmons frowned. "Better watch out, Doc. This Riley Harper would not only go by Simon Crutchfield's grave, he'll whistle Dixie while doing so."

"Whatcha mean?"

"Harper and Crutchfield were best friends. Crutchfield died under mysterious circumstances and then Harper married his wife within a year. She was his fifth, I think; I can't recall."

"Do you think he did it?"

"I don't think so. It was a long time ago, though, way before DNA. I wonder, but I don't think so. He has a reputation as a ruthless businessman, but I don't think he's that bad. I'll never forget him trying to stiff Bull on that old Impala. Man, the cat could afford to buy the dealership, and then to stop payment on a five-hundred-dollar check. He shoulda put his mama in better wheels anyway."

"Yeah, but he doesn't mind spending your tax dollars," Bones said.

"How's that?"

"Believe me, he'll do anything to keep Sandhills out of Harvey County. Last year they were gonna put an urgent care right to y'alls east; just west of Croatan County, and Harper got the facility Certificate of Need blocked in the legislature."

"Why'd he do that? We could use one. The ERs are always jammed."

"Yep, and all those patients get routed to Raleigh if Harvey Memorial can't take care of them. And those are usually the big money cases, you know, heart or neurosurgery. Harper was afraid some of those referrals out of the urgent care facility might drift east to Sandhills, so he put on the pressure. You can be sure they weren't gonna give up all those open-heart cases. The money is in those heart and trauma cases and Riley Harper was gonna have no part of not keeping his paws on that trickle. As the old saying goes: 'There's something wrong here, and it's got something to do with money.'"

"So how'd Harper stop it?" Rupert asked.

"Harper's backed Senator Rich Walton with CMA funds for years. He told Walton if he didn't keep Sandhills out of the area, he'd see to it all those funds dried up. Worked like magic. Didn't even get written up in the paper. Walton was chair of a Senate Committee on state medical services, and got it squashed so it never got out of committee."

"How'd you find out?" Rupert asked.

"Snookers Molesby knew a girl up there."

Rupert laughed. "Snook knows a girl everywhere. You still play golf with him?"

"Yeah, have since Harvey High School days."

"I don't think I'd let too many people know Snook talked."

"Don't worry. He's been my ace informant for years and he shoots straight without fail. I'll never out him."

They finished their meal and talked over the bluegrass gossip. Bones checked his watch. "I guess I better go. I'm gonna meet Dee and Lucas at CMA in a half hour."

"Again, watch out."

"Will do. Hey, Phispy is on the lookout for a used CRV for my daughter. If either one of you guys run across one, I'd like to look at it. We'd love to get one with twenty to thirty thousand miles and good service records."

"I'll watch out for one. I gotta tell ya, though, the used ones are hard to come by. People tend to hold onto 'em. I'll make you a deal if I get a low-mileage one in."

"Just think of me like a sheep, Rupert. It's okay to shear me, that way I can come back when I grow some more wool."

"Yeah, well, Riley'll try to skin you."

"I understand."

"Good. Don't forget," Simmons advised.

Chapter Nine

The meeting was in the CMA Board Room in Raleigh. Mr. Harper was a stout man in a fancy charcoal suit with light gray pinstripes. His black shoes were polished to a mirror shine. He had a partner with him, a Mr. Andrews, an angular, pasty figure who frowned the whole time.

Dr. Lucas passed a note to Dr. Dee. *Looks constipated.*

Bones looked down at his own flannel shirt and brogans. *I'm sure this man thinks I'm a rube,* he thought.

Harper went through a detailed Power Point slide show projection about all the benefits of the organization. As far as the docs could tell, not a single slide was about patient care. Bones nodded off.

Harper finally closed. "Any questions at this point?"

"Not really." Dee waved his hand. "Move on."

"Our doctors are very satisfied." Harper got out his pointer and backed up a couple slides. "Let me go back to this stat." He backtracked a few slides. "Okay, here is our annual provider survey." He flashed up the numbers. "Ninety-eight percent approval rating of CMA policies and procedures by our primary care providers."

Heck, fire, Bones thought. *I heard about that one even thought it was supposed to be anonymous. Everyone knew the pages were encoded so administration could trace it back. No way those docs were gonna speak their mind.*

Bones raised his hand. "Can you go back to the one about the first year's compensation package?"

Harper checked his watch. "Yes." He brought the slide back up.

Bones looked it over. "Just eyeballing that, you'd think that works out to be less for us than what we make now. I mean, we're veterans of almost twenty-five years. At what we make now, the young people aren't gonna come here. Less; no chance. I'm not mercenary, but we bring a lot to the table."

"You bring a lot? My understanding is that is not the case. Dr. Robertson, you're like all these other doctors. What you have is an outdated cottage industry product. You are more antiquated than a mom and pop grocery store."

Bones recalled when the old Tillman's grocery used to extend credit 'til pay day.

Harper went on. "We'd be glad to help you modernize. Do you want to be a part of the CMA family or not?"

Bones thought about that. *Whenever these guys started talking family you'd better watch out. It didn't fit his definition of the concept. To them it meant you either go along no questions asked or we'll crush you.* "We might, but we'll have to evaluate it all. Let me ask you something. Has Dr. Bill Greene been pretty happy?"

"That is not our practice. We manage it on a lease but it is not our preferred arrangement, and was a mistake we do not wish to repeat. Besides, Marvin Stanley found it too much trouble and can't take on another practice."

Too much local say-so, CMA's not skimming enough profit, Bones thought. "You know, I agree with you about family. I think Bill Greene felt that way, too. He couldn't bear to bolt to Sandhills. It seems his hybrid arrangement allows some control to rest with Harvey Memorial."

Andrews sipped his water, and frowned. Harper left his slide presentation and took a seat at the table.

Bones went on. "As these things evolve, it seems to me the local hospital has an even more vested interest in buying us than you guys in Raleigh would, just because they depend on us every day to provide patient care, and young people are not lined up to help us in these rural areas. Perhaps Harvey Memorial could offer a modification of the compensation package to reflect that need to keep us on board. Part of the 'family,' you know. Just like Dr. Greene."

Andrews sputtered out his water, and Harper fell out of his seat. His legs flailed wildly as he tumbled to the floor.

The doctors rushed to his side, but Harper dusted himself off. "Just slipped. I'm okay." Bones extended a hand. Harper brushed him away. "Don't touch me."

"Whatever." *I ain't a heathen,* Bones thought.

Harper took his seat again and cleared his throat. "Dr. Robertson, you must never mention such a concept again. If Pete Stark heard that he would have you put in jail. Compensation in exchange for referral of patients is forbidden by federal law."

"I understand. And that wasn't what I asked. I'll take it under advisement, though. I know the government is short on prison doctors; they might draft me if they project too severe a manpower shortage."

"Yes, they might indeed."

"So where do we go from here?" Bones asked.

"Are you interested?" Harper asked.

"I don't know. You haven't given us enough information. We haven't given you enough, either. Don't you think you guys ought to look the practice over?"

"That is not necessary."

"We won't go any further, then."

Harper put up his briefcase. "Humph. If you insist, we can arrange that."

"Good. I'll have our people get up with yours."

Harper shook hands with each doctor. Andrews followed him out of the room and never said a word.

The three doctors went over the meeting when they were out in the parking lot.

"Damn," Dee said, "I thought he'd coded when he fell outta that chair."

"I thought so, too," Lucas said.

"Did y'all catch the body language? He sure didn't want the commoners to lay hands on him, did he?" Bones had to laugh.

"No kidding." Dee shook his head.

"Where do you think it'll go?" Lucas asked.

"I have no idea, but we gotta follow the road. We know we're gonna play out in about three or four years, so we have time. No need to be rash yet," Bones said.

Bones did wonder, though. *How are we ever gonna negotiate with these guys? This is going to be like dealing with the Mafia.*

Chapter Ten

Simmons Rupert called Bones the week of the show. "Doc, you gonna be in for the Brownie Scott gig?"

"Yeah, boy. Promised Kate we'd take in Big Ed's. Can you join us?"

"Sure. You won't believe who came by Bluegrass Motors yesterday."

"Who's that?"

"Riley Harper."

Bones laughed. "His mama's Impala bite the dust?"

"Nope. The guy heard I knew some players and wanted to get some information about banjos."

"Banjos? What does he know about banjos?"

"Apparently very little. He said Lester Flatt played this one a few years ago."

"Lester on the banjo? Good Lord. Harper's all tangled up. Lester's been gone for decades. Harper musta had him confused with Earl."

"I guess. Anyway, he brought the banjo and wanted to trade it on a car. Said it was a pre-war flathead."

"Original?"

"He claims so; he made my insurance agent fax over a statement of coverage before he'd leave it with me. Anyway, I'm not sure what this means, but I thought I'd get Brownie to check it out."

The intercom at Bluegrass Motors blared away, "Customer to the showroom, customer to the showroom . . ."

"Gotta go, Doc."

"Hm. Can't wait to see what she says. We'll be there. See ya."

"Okay."

Brownie put it on at the show, and played two fine sets. Her new number, "Cotton Land," brought the house down. She signed autographs for an hour and then Bones, Kate, and Simmons visited backstage. Bones knocked on the dressing room door. "Hey, kid, ya'll decent in there?"

Brownie Scott opened the door and hugged Bones around the neck. "Doc? How in the world are ya? Lordy Kate, so good to see you."

"Great show, Brownie," Bones said. "Hey, you know Mr. Rupert here, don't you?"

"Sure. Good to see you, Simmons. Ya'll come on in."

Simmons Rupert toted along the banjo. "Mind looking at one?"

"Sure; love banjos." Brownie put on her readers.

Simmons put the case across the arms of the chair in the dressing room. "A guy wants to do a trade; the banjo for a late-model Mercedes. He claims this is an original pre-war five-string flathead."

Brownie's eyebrows went up and she peered over her glasses. "Hm. You don't see one of those very often. Open it up."

Simmons opened the case and handed the instrument to her.

She played a few bars of "Reuben." "Earl's first three-finger number," she said. Bones watched as her fingers raced over the fret board; they were slender and delicate but squeezed out a perfect cascade of powerful tones.

"Opinion?" Simmons asked.

Brownie hesitated to choose her words. "Well, this is a nice instrument. It plays well, but it isn't an authentic pre-war."

"How sure are you?" Simmons asked.

"Very confident. Look at the neck. See the inlay? It's hearts and flowers all right, but too even. These look like they were cut by the modern automated computer programs, not a human being. No way that is pre-war. Computer-cut programs do yield precision, but somehow the art and the charm just doesn't seem the same. And, too, these inlays are a bit larger than true pre-war. And the inlay at the first fret is a dead giveaway: The inlay started at the third fret on all the pre-wars."

"Wait a minute," Bones said. "My boy has a Scruggs repro and it has a first fret inlay. Earl's banjo was a pre-war Gibson and the company says the repro version is spot on for his."

"It is that. Legend has it one time Earl had it re-fretted, they gouged the fret board at the first fret so they put in an inlay as a fix. Don't know that for a fact, though." Brownie picked out a few bars of "Earl's Breakdown." "But like I said, it plays nicely. Just isn't pre-war." She looked it over again. "The original five strings had little nubs on the tension hoop." She rubbed her hand across the hoop. "Besides, no way this metal or the wood is that old." She picked a few more licks. "Good sound. Not pre-war, though. You can always tell. They can't be faked."

She laid it down, took off the resonator, and smelled the inside of the pot assembly. "Yep, the nitrocellulose lacquer hasn't aged out yet; can't be more than a decade old. It's a repro, no doubt. See the label? Looks real, but it doesn't line up right. The old ones aligned to perfection." She looked over the rim. "The serial number isn't stamped in the rim or the headstock either one; that's the way they marked 'em back then. And they always chalked the serial number in the resonator on the pre-war Gibsons. Not here." She placed the resonator back on the banjo, began to turn the thumb bolts, and looked at the inlays again. "Nice work there, but no yellow around the edges. Not even thirty years old."

Simmons was an old horse trader and car dealer. He got right to the heart of the matter. "Appraisal?"

Brownie smiled. "Well . . . as they say on 'Antiques Road Show,' if this were an authentic pre-war original five-string flathead it would be worth a hundred Gs."

"But as a trade on a Mercedes?"

Brownie laughed. "I know you know the answer. I regret to inform you, but even as fine a reproduction as this is, I would not recommend a trade for a Mercedes. Let me show you a real one." She opened her case. "Sonny wants me to record with this one." She ran through a few lines of "Rocky Top." "As one of my lawyer friends says, they are self-

authenticating. It's the sound. You know it when you hear it."
She ran over a few more bars. "It can't be duplicated."

Bones laughed. "I gotta tell ya, Brownie, you're right. I
can hear it. Can't make it sound like you do, but yeah, I can
hear it for sure. My friend Moose Dooley says if you play one
of these on the right moonlight night you might just cure
cancer."

Brownie smiled as she played. "I believe it."

"Hm. You better not quote me until I can get a journal
article."

"Just because it isn't science doesn't mean it isn't true,
Doc."

"I agree kid, I agree." Bones rubbed his chin. "I wonder
why in the world Riley Harper got interested in banjos all of
sudden. Hm. Well, Brownie Scott, you're a fine young'un.
You tell that John Wayne Scott that Doc said hello."

"Will do, Bones. Y'all take care."

Chapter Eleven

Peg paged Bones just before lunch. "Dr. Robertson? There's a lady on line two for you. Says she's Riley Harper's secretary."

"Okay." Bones picked up the phone. "Hello?"

"Yes. Dr. Robertson? Mr. Harper would like to arrange a meeting to evaluate your practice. He would prefer one evening in the next few weeks."

"Yes, ma'am. Just not on a Wednesday. It'd interfere with band practice."

"Pardon?"

"Oh, never mind. How 'bout Thursday the twelfth?"

She checked Harper's calendar. "Yes, that should be fine. Oh, one more thing, Dr. Robertson. I think Mr. Harper does hope to sign you." She stopped for moment then spoke in a whisper. "Don't tell him I said it, though."

"He wants to keep it in the family?"

"Yes."

"Well, that's good. Tell him one more thing, though. It ain't just me; he's got to sign all three docs and the staff, too. We're like musicians; thick as thieves."

"Sir?"

Bones suppressed a laugh. "Tell him the twelfth is fine. Seven-thirty, okay?"

"Yes, sir."

Harper was there at 7:30 sharp in his black Porsche on the night of the meeting. Dee and Lucas were there on time also. They got out of their cars to wait at the door.

Fifteen minutes passed.

"Is Dr. Robertson not coming?" Harper called out from his car.

Dee looked at his watch. "He'll be along. It's Fair week. He probably went to the pig races."

"Pig races? Egad." Harper's breath poured out into the chill. "Can't you let us in?"

"Sorry. Bones has the key."

"My lord."

Lucas chuckled. "The man has no idea what he's up against," she whispered.

Dee nodded. "Bones won't let up on him; I won't, either."

Directly Bones arrived. "Good God." Dee laughed out loud. "He's driving that hot rod of James Junior's."

It was a '74 Camaro, Carolina blue, fender skirts, shorty headers, dual exhaust and powered by a 350 with Chevy small block 30 bore over. Bones pulled up alongside Harper's

Porsche. The muscle car idled with a lurch then settled into a rhythmic muscle-car rocking motion.

Harper rolled down his window. "Turn that thing off!"

"Sorry, what'd ya say?" Bones flipped the ignition off.

"I said *turn that thing off!*" Harper shouted. His voice echoed through the night air.

"Man, you don't have to yell. We can hear."

Harper opened the door and lumbered out. Bones noticed a young woman in the passenger seat. She was blond, sort of a Twiggy type, well at least most of her was of that physique, and couldn't have been a third of Harper's age. Harper leaned over and kissed her full on the mouth.

"See you, sweetie," she said.

Harper grunted some kinda guttural noise. "Beep me in one hour if I'm not out, Ginger."

"Yes, sir."

They made their way to the door. He turned to Ed Dee and smiled. "You got the key?"

"Nope. Gave it to you."

Bones fished around in his pockets. "Here we go." Bones turned the key and they stepped inside. Harper rubbed his hands. Bones checked the thermostat. "We'll turn up the heat, Mr. Harper. Gotta save on the power bill, you know. Sorry I'm late. We ran the rod in the drag race at the fair. Had to wait 'til Alison Brown's set was over, though. Never in all my born days have I seen a show that could shut down the pig races. Why that little California surfer girl is a better draw than the Demolition Derby."

"I'm impressed." Harper grunted again. "Where can we sit down and discuss the issues?" Harper asked.

"We'll have to use the waiting room. We don't have a conference room and the break room is a little small. Can I get you anything to eat?"

"No, thanks."

"Too bad. You oughta try these vinegar fries. They've got 'em out at the fair." Bones offered him a paper funnel cup with a few fries left in the bottom.

"No, thanks."

They all sat down in the waiting room.

Harper began. "Well, again to take up where we left off at our last meeting, we do have interest and would like to help you. Mr. Andrews has run some preliminary numbers based on the financial statements you forwarded. How interested are you?"

"Good Lord, Mr. Harper, we have no idea." Bones finished the last of the fries and tossed the cup away. "I mean, you haven't even seen the practice. We've been here twenty years."

"It shows. You don't have much of a location."

"Location? How could it be better? We're right across from the school house, and we get all kinda young people. We're the fourth doctor's office here, and every one of them has been a success. That magnolia tree out front was planted by the Huggins family right after the Civil War. There's a lot of history here."

Harper yawned.

Bones went on. "It's a great location. The rescue squad is only a block away. When you have a code they are spot on; my boy's a paramedic in the squad. Flies the chopper, too, but not to us; no need with them this close."

"Very nice."

Bones began to raise his voice. "Heck fire, Mr. Harper, if you have a bad day we're only two blocks from the ABC store. It's right across the street from 'Liquor View' Apartments."

Lucas rolled her eyes and smiled.

"Location, location, location . . . ." Harper scribbled a note.

"For heaven's sake, you haven't even looked at our equipment or even our furniture." Bones began to raise his voice.

"Hm. I suppose we could make some adjustments. All this is depreciated out, but well let's see . . . . Hm. There are fifteen chairs in this room. At five dollars a chair—"

Bones jumped out of his seat. "Man, what's wrong with you? Don't you want to hear about our patients or our staff? They are the best. I don't want to talk about chairs. Don't you care about our vision?"

"Dr. Robertson, if you had vision you wouldn't need us." Harper flashed a wry smile.

Dee intervened. "I understand, Mr. Harper. My sister is an accountant. We realize these things have to be grounded in solid business considerations. I think all Bones, uh, Dr. Robertson is trying to say is there is more to medicine than business. Good will is a major factor, especially in primary care."

"We don't take it into consideration. Even if we did, the Stark law would not allow it. Good will is an antiquated concept."

"That's obvious," Bones muttered.

"Beg your pardon?" Harper asked.

"Never mind." Bones stood up. "Tell you what, Mr. Harper. I need to get back over to the fairgrounds. The pig races are on in a half hour and Alison has a second set at ten. You run some more numbers and get back to us."

Riley Harper stood up and served up a fish-limp handshake. "We will, Dr. Robertson. I assure you we will give you the best offer allowed by law. Everyone who has signed with us is happy. Just ask Dr. Blake."

"I'll do that."

They escorted him to the back door. Bones turned the thermostat back down, set the alarm, and locked up. They watched as Harper drove away. Bones went back to his desk to get his pipe, and walked back down the stairs. "Arrogant rascal, huh?"

"Yep," Dee replied.

"I believe I'll go to negotiation school," Janie Lucas commented. "All you gotta do is learn three dumb statements and then say them over and over until the other side gives up; doesn't matter what the question is."

"Yep. They hide behind that Pete Stark guy like he was their mama. See you guys in the morning." Bones walked over to the Camaro, climbed in, and rolled down the window. "I'm gonna go catch Alison's set and try to calm down." The muscle car turned over on the third crank, and Bones rumbled off.

Chapter Twelve

A proposal arrived from Riley Harper in two weeks via certified mail. The three doctors met over lunch.

"So, guys, what do you think?" Bones asked.

Dee thumbed through the document. "I've never looked over one of these before, but it seems we would have been better off to start a hardware store twenty years ago."

Lucas lay her papers on the desk. "What's wrong with these guys? They only give you part of the equation and expect an answer. There's not a word in here about the employment contracts after year one."

"Exactly." Bones agreed. "If they pay us for the practice and then extract it back out of us over time, then that was just a short-term loan."

"With exorbitant interest. You know what?" Lucas asked. "You own the real estate. Was that issue addressed at all?"

"Not that I could see." Bones started to put his copy in his briefcase, and a line caught his eye. He laughed out loud.

"What's so funny?" Dee asked.

Bones slid the paper across the desk. "Take a look at page thirteen. Check out the line item under 'liabilities.' That's where they plugged you in, pal. Don't feel bad, me and Lucas are listed there, too."

Dee flashed a wry smile. "Liabilities. I get it."

Bones picked up the document and placed it in his briefcase. "The purchase price is about twenty cents on the dollar, at least if our accountant was even in the ballpark. I wonder if they left off a zero! Obviously, we can't have an opinion on this yet. I'll give 'em a call."

Bones called Harper at lunch, and got his secretary. "Yes, ma'am. James Robertson here. Is Mr. Harper in?"

"No, he's at the state senate hearings on healthcare delivery systems. His son is a pioneer in electronic medical records."

"I'll bet. When will he be back?"

"Oh, next week. Can I help you?"

"Yes, ma'am. Oh, let me ask you something. You guys have any notion whether the new healthcare legislation will make electronic medical records mandatory?"

"Hm. I don't know. I'm sure it is the way of the future, though."

"I have no doubt." Bones thumbed through the practice proposal. "Anyway, we received Mr. Harper's proposal, and uh, well . . . was some of it missing?"

"How do you mean?"

"We looked it over very carefully. It made an offer on the practice, but didn't address ongoing contractual issues. It made no mention of real estate considerations, either."

"Oh, that is standard policy for our acquisitions. There is no reason to spend the time or the money for real estate appraisals if there is not genuine interest. Have you signed the proposal yet?"

"Signed it? Ma'am, we can't possibly sign it until we know what we are signing. I own the building. How can I tell you I'll sell it to you if you won't make me an offer on it?"

"We just don't do it that way."

"Well, I do. Heck, my mama would have the courtesy to tell me what she was gonna pay me for a car before she'd ask me to sign over the title. Mr. Harper needs to talk to Phipsy-the-honest-used-car dealer. We're straight up with each other."

"Who?"

"Oh, never mind." Bones paused for a moment. "Oh, well, it doesn't matter for now anyway. The offer on the practice was way too low to even consider. I'm sure we'll propose some sort of counteroffer."

"Dr. Robertson, Capital Medical Acquisitions is the premier physician organization in the state. Mr. Harper and CMA made you the best offer allowed by Federal law. A counter will not make him happy. I am certain he'll be quite insulted."

"Oh, well. Maybe that's a good thing."

"Sir?"

"Look ma'am. I'm sure you're a nice lady, and I know you've gotta say what they teach you to say at negotiation school. CMA does have a great group of docs, and we want to be a part of it, but we need more information. I'll talk it over with my people."

"I'll tell him you have the offer under consideration."

"Whatever."

Bones relayed the conversation to Dr. Dee at the office. "So, boss, what do you think?"

"Ah, they're just doing the business dance. You're the type to give people a straight answer on the first pass-through. They never do it that way."

"What should we do?"

"Okay to run it by my sister? She's the accountant."

"Okay with me, if it's okay with Lucas."

Dee had an answer by Friday. They met at Chang's Chinese. "I guess we did okay for amateurs. Sis agrees: We don't have enough information. She says to look at this thing like a three-legged stool."

The server put some hot tea on the table. "Buffet and bluegrass wonton?" he asked.

"Yes, sir," Bones answered.

"Only in Harvey County." Dee smiled. "Bring me a bowl, too; our usual." The server went to get their soup. They took in the buffet and sat back down.

"A three-legged stool? How's that?" Bones asked.

"One leg is the acquisition price, the second is the ongoing yearly contract for physician compensation, and the third is real estate," Dee explained. If you agree to one part at a time they'll just whittle away on the other legs. If one leg is too long they'll chop off part of one of the other ones until they're satisfied."

"Just like big biz or big government either one; first they break your legs, then they offer you a crutch so you can hobble."

"And ask you to pay for it *and* smile, at that. She says an offer of sixty-three grand for any three-doctor practice, especially one as busy as ours, is a ridiculous low ball on leg number one. She believes the practice is worth at least three or four times that. They've got to be kidding."

"Well, that's what I thought, too, but it's not my field of expertise. Would she be willing to draw up a counter-proposal? We'd be glad to pay her for her time."

"Consider it done. All she asks for is one free gig from the band." Dee sipped on his tea.

"Man, these chicken wings rock." Bones tossed one aside. The server brought their soup. "Bluegrass wonton; just wonton with white rice." He took a sip. "Someday it's gonna catch on. Sis got any other advice?"

"She agrees with your three-year deadline, but on another front. Come Y2K our computers will not move forward. They'll think the year is nineteen hundred instead of two thousand. They'll have to be replaced. It's another expense to consider. It'd be best if we could get a deal done a year or so before that deadline. Otherwise we'd go through the expense and trouble of a new computer system only to have it ditched when new management mandated a change to their data base, which they will."

"Hm. Planned obsolescence. The biz guys always set it up that way. I'll bet Harper's boy has just the electronic medical records computer solution for us, and it'd only cost us fifty grand."

Dee laughed. "Yep. I'll tell Sis to factor that in. I'm gonna get some more moo-goo-gai-pan." Dee got up to go back to the buffet.

"Get me a few wings." Bones poured up another hot tea.

Chapter Thirteen

There was little fanfare when Billy joined the practice that fall.

Bones showed him around the office the weekend he was to start working there. Billy passed by a single white phone on the wall by the lab. "What's this one for, Doc? Perhaps your direct line to the Soviets?"

"You're close, Billy. We call it the secret line. We occasionally use it in the event of an emergency if the regular phone lines are down. We almost never give out the number. It only rings about every ten years. The first time it rang it was Dr. Rubencoff in Raleigh; I was early on in my practice. I picked it up and he said is this Dr. Robertson?"

"Yes it is."

"This is Dr. Rubencoff."

"Yes sir."

"Do not ever send your patient Mrs. Massingill to me again. Her heart is too bad. I can not help her. No one can help her."

"Uh, yes, sir. I promise. It's just no one is supposed to die of heart disease in Harvey County unless we've had you check 'em out."

"Whatever. Do not send her again."

"Yes, sir."

Bones turned to Billy. "Yeah, when Rubencoff called it might as well have been the Soviets. I was scared to death of him. Anyway, the line doesn't ring often and when it does it is usually someone important."

"Got it."

"So, you want to go to Chang's for lunch?" Bones asked.

"Sure, that'd be great."

They placed their orders as soon as they got to Chang's and settled in for a little chit-chat.

"Are you ready to start to work Monday?" Bones asked.

"Yes, sir."

Bones sipped on his hot tea. "Man, I'm like Indie. Once we get that first frost I 'bout go into hibernation." He looked over at Billy. "Look, kid. We're tickled to have you and you're gonna do fine."

"I hope so."

"Sure you will. You're well trained, you care; it's all good."

Billy took a bite out of his egg roll. "One time I heard about a doc who started out in a little town; a place about like Harvey County. The town's mayor had a heart attack the first day the doctor was on the job. The mayor died, and the doc about did, too. This guy never got over it. He went back to the university to teach."

Bones twisted his moustache. "When I started out I was so naïve I thought if I read enough books and cared enough, none of my patients would ever die. It just doesn't work that way." He scratched his gray whiskers. "I wish it did. Sometimes I'll go over to the graveyard in the spring to put roses on Indie's grave. I'll walk through there at dusk and see all those old patients who we finally ran outta cards on. It's kinda discouraging but all we can do is our best."

Billy looked out the window. "Hey, Doc, it's like you say, 'I'll do all my crying before the time.'"

"Dang right, Billy. I cry at funerals but not once has it been 'cause I was worried about what I should have done. When they lay 'em in the ground ain't the time to rethink your diagnosis. Do it ahead of time every time." Bones thought back to a funeral. "Hey, there was this funeral; it was for a favorite patient. The preacher warbled, 'He's gone and the doctors didn't even know he had heart trouble.'" I almost jumped out of my seat. I wanted to say, 'Wait a dang minute, Preacher. I knew he had heart trouble, but the rascal didn't show for his treadmill and I didn't get a second chance. It ain't my fault.' I held my peace, though.

"After the funeral several folks came up to me in private, and said, 'Doc, we know what happened. It ain't your fault. He was old and sick and just ready to move on.'" Bones thought back to the events and rubbed his eyes. "Contact lenses are bothering me, kid. Anyway, that one still hurts to this day." Bones looked up at the ceiling. "I still wonder if he'd gone for his treadmill if I coulda eked out another couple years for him. I'm gonna ask God when I get to Heaven. Anyway, you're right. Do all your crying ahead of time as best you can, Billy. When they are in the grave and when you want to think up one last thing that mighta helped."

'I will, Doc. I don't know if I live up to your reputation or not."

"You'll do better. Y'all know a lot more than we did. You remember when I used to come to talk to y'all at the Harvey High Medical Explorer Club? My hair was as black as yours. When we were coming along we didn't have as much help. It's sorta like when we learned to play music. Back when I was a kid we scratched up a bunch of records to learn all those licks. Now there's all kinda great instruction at your fingertips. The kids are better players than we were. It'll be the same for you as a doctor. There's a lot more support."

"I don't know; there's nothing like experience."

"And nothing like passing it on. Tap into it at every opportunity, son." Bones chomped on a chicken wing. "Know this for a fact: If there's any trouble, I'm there for you, and I've seen some."

"Your record is clean."

"Yeah, but it's only by the Grace of God and good luck. I dodged a few close calls. I learned a lot from Indie. You will, too."

"How's that?"

"Always put the patient first. You can't go wrong if you do that." Bones cast his eyes skyward. "Don't forget, God and Indie watch over us."

"Will do, Doc."

Bones reached over and picked up Billy's check. "One last time on the 'Starving Medical Student Foundation.' After you get your first paycheck, we're doing Dutch."

Billy smiled. "Okay."

Chapter Fourteen

The doctors arranged a conference call with Dr. Dee's sister after she'd had a few more weeks to go over a second run-through on the documents.

"So, Sis. What do you think?" Dee asked.

"First, I want you to tell all the doctors this is not my area of expertise. Most of my experience is in the financial services industry. That said, though, I don't see how you can accept this at face value. I have several recommendations . . . ."

After her input, the doctors agreed on a modest counterproposal. Bones looked it over. "Looks okay to me. Three-fifty is still well below our accountant's original appraisal. Fair market for the real estate. We might have to tweak the on-going yearly employment contracts some more; I don't know. I want to give them every chance to be reasonable. After all, we've been in this medical community for twenty-five years and I want to co-operate if I'm given any chance to. I don't want to make a change unless they force us to."

The other docs agreed. They forwarded the counter proposal to Riley Harper and waited.

Riley Harper replied in two weeks. The call was terse. "We have already forwarded our best offer. Stark law precludes any further discussion. When shall we draw up the documents? We know you are anxious to move forward. We anticipate a professional working relationship. We will fax confirmation; formal documentation will follow."

Bones did his best to stifle a laugh. "I'll take it under advisement."

He retrieved the fax and took it to his partners. "Is this guy crazy or what?"

Dee read it over. "Man, I don't think he even looked at what we had to say."

Lucas didn't bother to read it. "If you guys aren't satisfied, I'm sure I'm not either. Where do we go from here?"

Bones tossed the document on his desk. "I'm not sure. Let me make some contacts. I promise you this much; they view this as a game of attrition. They know quite well every primary care physician in North Carolina is on the ropes. They have both the power and the money. This is like the siege of Vicksburg. They view it as they have time on their side, and we have no way out."

"They might be right," Lucas countered.

"Maybe so. Give me some time to think on it."

Bones put his feet up on his desk. He recalled the story of Arthur Smith when Hollywood tried to use "Dueling Banjos" in the movie *Deliverance* and not pay the music royalties. So the legend goes the big city lawyers said, "We're big. You are little. You don't have the time or the money to fight us." Arthur replied, "Well, we might be little and we don't have the money, but we've got plenty of time."

It lasted several years, but Arthur got his day in court. The judge heard it all out, and called all the parties into his chambers. He addressed the corporate lawyers first. "Gentlemen, to me this is very clear. There is no doubt; this is his song. I suggest you appease him." They agreed to hear it out; they had no choice. The Judge turned to Mr. Smith. "Sir, if I could, may I ask if you would please tell these gentlemen what you want?"

And Arthur, in that South Carolina twang that was a perfect match to his precision guitar picking, said, "Everything it made."

And from what Bones understood, that's about what he got. Bones smiled. Arthur finished first in his high school class and turned down an appointment at the Air Force Academy to pursue a career in music with his guitar. *Never underestimate a picker,* Bones thought.

Bones put in a call to hospital VP Chick Crawley. "You got time to play golf Wednesday?"

"Sure, what's on your mind?"

"Hospital biz. Put it on their tab."

"Serious talk?"

"Yep."

"Who else is gonna be there?"

"Just Snook."

"You got a pigeon lined up?"

"Nah, just a friendly game, that's all."

"Okay."

Chick and Bones rode in the cart. Snook knew they had business to tend to, so he elected to walk. "I'm in training anyway, Bones. Need the exercise." Snook headed towards the first tee.

Bones smiled. "Okay. Chick, let me ask you something," Bones said. "What do you know about this Riley Harper out of Raleigh?"

Chick looked around to be sure Snookers was out of earshot. "He's a turd. Don't say I said it, though."

"What dealings have you had with him?"

"Dr. Greene's practice."

"What happened?"

"Harper tried to steal it from Greene."

"So I hear."

"Yep, Sandhills almost got to the table. If I hadn't brokered a compromise we coulda lost Dr. Greene to the eastern front. It was almost a major error."

"How did it play?"

"In truth, Stanley knew the implications were and he was relieved that I managed to salvage the market share. But Harper was pissed; he doesn't like having his authority undermined. Stanley had to act like the deal made him mad, too, to save his job. I guess he had to. Raleigh has the lease on Harvey Memorial and they demand our referrals." Chick jotted down the scores for the last few holes. "It woulda been Marvin's job if Riley thought he wasn't co-operating. It was damn near mine. I took the blame, but I got to keep my job. Stanley promised Harper he would discipline me and it wouldn't happen again."

"Strange cats, I tell you." Bones shook his head. "Someday Sandhills will find a way to break into the market here. If Harper refuses to negotiate, it might well be with our practice. We could be the ones to break rank. I always want to be part of the solution for the community, but I won't let Raleigh take advantage of me or my people, either one. Indie taught me better than that."

Chick got out of the cart, set up, and hit his wedge shot on the green. "Hell, Bones. We don't want to lose you. I know Stanley talks all that family crap, but for me and you, it's real. We've always been able to talk turkey."

"I agree."

"You've been our number one provider for a quarter century. We need to work out a deal."

"You might better convince Marvin Stanley. Harper's hopeless."

"Give me some time," Chick replied. "Do you have an appraisal?"

"Yep. It was by our accountant, so I guess they'll argue it's informal and not arm's length. I bet it'll be close, though. He knows where every dime went over the years, and some of them were pretty thin."

"I understand. Follow the money. Better get an official one by a certified commercial and medical practice appraiser. I'll be back in touch."

They got out of the cart and walked to the green. Snook caught up and putted out for a birdie.

"How 'bout a burger, Bones?" Chick asked.

"Sure."

"B and B okay?"

"Okay."

Snook patted Bones on the elbow. "Hey, brother, y'all got business to tend to and I have some errands to run. I'll be by after a while."

Chick extended a hand to Snook to shake. "Can you play the Member/Guest with me this year?"

"Sure," Snook said.

Bones and Chick drove to the B and B. When they walked in Minnie the Myna did the siren imitation and then uncorked a loud rooster crow. "Cockle-doodle-do!!!"

Chick laughed. "I guess I've graduated to a regular now."

"Yep," Lou said. Lou got them a table in the back private room and took their order.

Bones shifted in his chair. "Hope we can strike a deal, pal."

"Cautious optimism, Doc." Chick flashed a wry smile.

"With the emphasis on caution."

Chick nodded. "Are you aware of Dr. Yelton's situation?"

"The oncologist?"

"Correct."

"What's up with him? Great doctor. We sure need him in Harvey County."

Chick got up and closed the door, then came back to their table in the back room. "Yes, we do. I'm afraid we won't have him much longer."

"My goodness. Is he sick?"

"No, his health is fine. He just crossed Riley Harper."

"What happened?"

"He did some continuing education at Sandhills and got interested in their lymphoma protocols. The next thing you know CMA saw a drift in their referral patterns. Worked all the way up to sixty-three percent going to Sandhills Oncology; way too much market share for Harper's taste."

"I know Yelton. I'm sure he just did what he thought was best for his patients."

"No doubt in my mind. But it pissed Harper off. He told Yelton if he couldn't get his referral pattern right he was gonna terminate his lease at the cancer center."

"Good Lord."

"Yelton told him to take a hike; no administrator was gonna tell him where to refer his patients. So Riley terminated him effective April first."

"He's the best cancer doc we've ever had in Harvey County and the only one right now. Hell, even Olden wasn't that controlling." Bones slammed his hand on the table. "And all his big talk about excellence in patient care. Nothing but lip service. Now all our cancer patients will have to go out of town. Damn." Bones got up and paced around the room. "What was Harper thinking?"

"He said it was just business."

"Just business? What these biz guys don't get is this is a people biz, not a money biz. They try to turn it into a money biz and then the people go away. Then there's no money and they don't understand what happened. Dumb." Bones began to pace.

Chick laughed. "Settle down, Don Quixote." He pulled out Bones' seat. "Sit down, pal. You know what I think? There is no way a guy like you will be satisfied to work for Riley Harper, not that he's gonna cut you a fair deal anyway. Don't say I said it; it'd be my job."

"I understand."

Chick went on. "We need to keep you. Let me work out something like what we did with Greene. I'll make sure Marvin understands the stakes."

"Okay."

Chick and Bones shook hands, and Chick left. Minnie let out a loud wolf whistle. Snookers had just come in the door. "Hey, Snook. Bones is in the back. I know he'd love to see you," Chick said.

"Sure. Hey, Lou, how 'bout a PBR?" Snookers hollered to Lou.

Lou waved from behind the counter. "Sure 'nuff, Snook."

Snook went to the back room, waved at Bones, and took a seat. They shook hands. "You know what I think, Bones?"

"What's that?"

"Chick always adds up his score right."

"I agree. That has been my experience, anyway. They need to listen to Chick over there. He's the most honest one they've got."

"Know what else?" Snookers asked.

"What's that?"

"Chick's right. Harper's a turd."

Bones laughed. "Don't tell anyone."

"Want a beer?" Snook asked.

"Sure." Bones pulled out his pipe, filled the bowl with Granger Select, and sat back to think. "You know what, Snook? I think Harper already has his mind made up. If he stiffs us and we defect, it'll go down as the single biggest health care marketing strategy error in the history of Harvey County."

Snook furrowed his brow. "It'd be a whopper, no doubt. If I had the man's ear I'd say don't let your deal go down."

Riley Harper buzzed his secretary. "Ginger Snap, another pot of coffee."

"Yes, sir."

She brought it to his desk. "Have we heard anything more from Dr. Robertson?" Harper asked.

"No, sir."

"We will soon. He has no options. By God, I haven't got to where I am by negotiating with a hillbilly, and I'm not about to start now."

"Yes, sir."

He pulled his coat off the rack. "And please take this back to Mr. Hamilton. It is not tailored properly. Tell him I said I do not appreciate shoddy workmanship."

"Yes, sir."

"And get my mail. I'm behind."

"Yes, sir."

"Heathens . . . ."

"Sir?"

"Oh, never mind. Just get my mail, and put some damn sugar in my coffee."

"Yes, sir."

Chapter Fifteen

Charles Thombley was a negotiator. His people came from Atlanta, and he was raised there. All of the Thombley clan had an eye for a deal. They got their start in real estate futures right after Sherman came through Atlanta, then made wise investments and grew their fortune. They were interested in philanthropy and specialized in the assistance for small churches to acquire a solid, long-term financial strategy. Thombley had a head of salt-and-pepper wavy hair with pure gray in the temples that favored bluegrass star Del McCoury. He wore silk shirts and tailored suits, and was a minority shareholder in the Braves organization. Charles Thombley was of money.

But he had an ear for the traditional, too, and took in his share of bluegrass music.

Bones decided it was time for help, and called. "Charles, Bones here. When you gonna be through this way?"

"I have a meeting in Raleigh in three weeks. You got a show?"

"No, man, I might need your help."

"What's up?"

Bones brought him up to speed.

"My goodness. I hope you haven't signed anything."

"No, sir. I met with Chick some. I think he wants to make it happen, but he'll have to have a push from outside the system for us to be validated. We're not gonna be able to close the deal alone, at least not anything we can live with. Can you help us?"

"Sure, I can stop on the way."

"You good with Bee Bridges Barbecue?"

"Sure. You blue-grassers know where to find the best Q and coffee."

They met for an hour. Thombley thumbed through the documents.

"So, whaddaya think?" Bones asked.

The waitress brought their sandwiches. Charles turned the folder over and laid it to the side.

"Anything else, boys?" she asked.

"Yes, ma'am. I'd like some extra French fries," Bones said.

She left. Charles picked up the folder, and waved it at Bones. "I get so tired of these guys. Childish."

"What you mean?"

"Word on the street is Riley Harper isn't gonna be outdone by some hillbilly. This is all about ego and money, nothing else."

"Can you get a deal done?"

"Sure. Your daddy didn't raise a fool. You try to be fair, but you can get your back up if someone tries to take advantage of you. I'm surprised you didn't call before now. When is your next meeting with Chick?"

"Next Wednesday."

"Put it off a month. I can't get back 'til then. Don't tell him I'm coming until the last minute."

"Okay, boss. What's your game plan?"

"Here's the deal: Riley Harper knows you have to see patients, and don't have time to work on all this. He doesn't have anything else he has to do. He can afford to wait it out; he's got time on his side."

"Well, now *I've* got *you*."

"And now you also have time. Use it to your advantage. It'll worry them to no end that you're not in a hurry."

"It's strange, Charles, but even after the way they've treated us, I still want to carve out something with the home team if at all possible."

"I think that's wise, even though they are too slow to see it's in their best interest. I'll crunch the numbers and show 'em they can make money on a fair deal."

"You think they'll do it?"

Thombley tugged on his ear. "I don't know. They can be short-sighted at times, but I'll make it quite clear. If they let you get away, it will be a major error. Good Lord, you guys send more heart cases to Raleigh Cardiovascular than Cary Internal Medical does."

"Must be our barbecue." Bones waved to the waitress to order a sandwich to go. "They do make medicine to counter all that, but half the time the insurance companies won't cover it."

Charles looked at the contract again. "This won't do. I'll get 'em to see the light."

"If they don't they'll try to blame it on me; wait and see."

"Your place in the history book is secure, Doc. Indie saw to that. Don't let 'em bluff you."

"Okay."

Thombley ordered another pitcher of tea, and one last round of hush puppies. "Now as far as the word on the street, you always have the bluegrass beat covered."

Bones puffed out his chest. "Yeah, now in that world I know my people. Simmons Rupert and Bull Wilson have Raleigh covered. Brownie Scott comes through for a show every so often, and she brings up to speed on what's said afar. We'll be at her show next month."

"Good. Now, what do you know about horse-racing?"

"Next to nothing."

"Okay. Count on me for that. Keep a watch out for the Kentucky Derby Kid."

"Who's that?"

"A good contact."

"What does she look like?"

"Dark brunette hair, light mahogany skin, part Italian, part Latin, about twenty-five."

"Mercy, Charlie. Does your wife know you hang out with women who look like that?"

"Oh, she's harmless, but still I wouldn't travel with her. You probably won't ever see her. She works off the messenger model. Yeah, I haven't looked over the marriage license in a while but I'm certain my contractual arrangements with my wife do not allow for any such exclusionary clause as a Latino/Italian girl half my age to be a travel companion. I'm a good negotiator, but not that good."

"Kate wouldn't sign that contract, either, I assure you. It'd be mighty dark to travel for me right quick."

Charles went on. "Anyway, her code word in this acquisition will be Real Quiet."

"No problem. I know not to talk. I learned that in Indie's case."

"No, no, Bones. 'Real Quiet,' as in the horse. The Kentucky Derby Kid loves to play the ponies. She says Real Quiet is better than even odds on the Derby. So if you get the code word 'Real Quiet is a winner,' it means to go ahead with the deal."

"And sign?"

"Probably, but wait for me to call and confirm."

"Will do, boss. By the way, your code name from here on out is Del."

"As in McCoury?" Thombley asked.

"Yes. Best hair in bluegrass."

"Okay."

Chapter Sixteen

Brownie Scott was a determined little young'un. She was slight of build, a slender brunette from upstate South Carolina who played shortstop and center field for the boy's teams all the way through high school. The child was so focused she'd run right through a fence to snag a fly ball. Once she got on base, which was quite often, those Bambi legs would steal second more times than not. What she lacked in raw brute strength she more than made up for in finesse, speed, and quickness, and the girl possessed a pure baseball intelligence and intuition for the game that all the guys came to respect.

But even more than baseball, Brownie loved the banjo. Before she turned pro she was the sideman of choice for every jam session and semi-professional upstate gig. Nowadays she fronted her own band, "The Brownie Scott Quartet," and in a decade had already won The IBMA Banjo Player of the Year four times.

Brownie called Bones Monday morning. "Hey, Doc. Wish ya coulda made Kinston. We had a good gig, and pretty fair traffic at the record table."

"Cool. I hate I couldn't make it. I was on call; would have been there otherwise."

"Do you know a Kentucky Derby Kid?" Brownie asked. "They often just call her KDK."

"Never met her, but I've heard of her."

"She was at the show. Dark-haired girl like me. Had a nice late model RB3. Good banjo. It was a straight-up deal. She wanted eighteen-hundred, and I bought it for my cousin. He's gonna tour with Sparks this summer and had been looking for a working musician instrument. Anyway, KDK sent a message."

"I hear that's how she works. What's the message?"

"Real Quiet."

Bones held the phone to his ear with his shoulder and picked up a pen. "Time to deal already?"

"Nope. Just put your money on 'Real Quiet' in the Derby. Hold the message close 'til then. And don't sign until Del McCoury sings."

"Got it."

"Did you know KDK used to work for Sandhills?"

"Really?"

"Yep. She still has a lot of contacts down east. CEO Chevalier is interested in you guys; no doubt."

"Great."

"There's only one problem. He's in line for a cabinet position. He'll be in Washington in two years."

"And the impact on us?"

"The organization hates to lose him, but it'll be seamless. For one thing, it'll give you an insider in the Beltway. But all politics are local. Even more important, his replacement is already in line: Melinda Rose."

"Wild Irish?"

"Yep. Five foot, two inches tall, green eyes, got the fire inside. Fine Celtic fiddler, too. They both understand the need to create a medical home model. Believe me, you guys could be the ticket for Sandhills in Harvey County. Give them every chance."

"Hm." Bones tugged on his beard. "I don't have any problem with a lady CEO, but I'll talk to Billy, about it; sometimes the younger guys worry a woman might not be tough enough."

"She's tough."

"I have no fear. My Kate is tough and little Marie is, too. After I got to know Lucille Taggert, and you, too, for that matter, I never doubted women in assertive roles." Bones laughed. "Hey, did you read Newsweek about a month ago? There was an article about women in combat roles. The debate was whether or not women were suited for combat."

"Didn't see it. What did they say?"

"Check it out. You need to read it. After all, you're a woman who has succeeded in a man's world. When I was coming up, all the banjo players were old guys in coveralls who chewed tobacco. We're better off now that bluegrass isn't just a boy's club."

"So what did they conclude about women in combat?"

"As always, you learn more from the readers than anyone else. Some wag wrote in a couple weeks later and said he'd survived three divorces in California and after that he had no doubt women were well suited to combat."

Brownie laughed. "Well, The Kentucky Derby Kid says Wild Irish Rose is tough, too, so don't worry about signing and then having Chevalier split after you're on board. She'll be great, too. And KDK was honest on the RB3 banjo deal. My guess is you guys would be well served to check out what Sandhills has to offer. And one more thing: I'd get it done before Y2K."

"I agree on that. I can't afford the new computers, and besides, we're gonna have to go EMR, too. We can't handle it and make overhead."

"KDK says they have already begun to gear up at Sandhills, so they'll be ahead of that curve easy if you joined them," Brownie said.

"Yeah, so has CMA, but they'll use it as a club. Riley Harper knows dang good and well I can't afford the fifty grand it's gonna take to get the new system his son has recommended to the senate as the EMR computer record system of choice for all these dumb doctors who haven't kept up with the times. He's a sorry rascal! Hey, you won't be surprised that Riley Harper pulled some strings with Senator Walton and his boy has the exclusive East Coast distribution rights on the government's EMR of choice."

"Mercy. Oh, my. Okay, I'll pass the message on to Del McCoury."

"Mr. Thombley does favor him, huh?"

"Yep. Y'all play hard, and stay in touch."

Chapter Seventeen

Dee met with Bones on hospital rounds. "I called Sis. She said if Chick wanted a certified medical appraiser she'd get up with a Ms. Fountain." He handed Bones a note with a phone number. "She's over in Greensboro. It'd be worth the trip. She's got no ax to grind in this thing. Sis says she's a pro."

"Good. Thanks for the tip."

Dr. Dee sat down at the nurses' station and opened a chart, then looked up. "I hate for us to have to spend the money, but without a certified medical appraisal I'm afraid if we don't we've put Chick in a spot where he can't help us."

"I agree, Ed. Del had me put off the meeting a few weeks. It'll be time and money well spent. I gotta go over to ICU. A patient of mine is in a bad way over there. I'm just courtesy, and not the doc of record on the case, but I want to speak to the family. I'll see you at the office."

"Who's Del?" Dr. Dee asked.

"Oh that's my code name for Mr. Thombley. His hair looks just like Del McCoury's."

Ed smiled. "It does, huh? Okay."

Bones made the call. "Is Ms. Fountain in?"

"May I ask who's calling?"

"Bones Robertson."

"Oh, hey. Are you the doctor who plays bluegrass music?"

"That's me. One of 'em, anyway."

"When y'all gonna play the State Theater?"

"Hm. Dunno. They think bluegrass isn't quite sophisticated enough for 'em. We still gig at the Billiard and Bowl here in Harvey County."

"Who do they think they're gonna hire around here? The Vienna Boy's Choir?"

"I understand. Hey, we're booked to open for Darin and Brooke Aldridge over in the western part of the state, Shelby."

"I guess so; it's the home of Earl Scruggs and Don Gibson. They know real music there."

"Don't worry. The rest of the world will catch on. What you got on your mind?"

"I need to talk to Ms. Fountain about an appraisal."

"Let me get her for you."

Fountain came to the phone and heard Bones out. "Appraisal? So you want to sell your practice?"

"It's not that I want to, but, yeah, sometime in the next couple years I'm afraid we'll have to. We can't compete."

"The trend is great for my business, but I'm not so sure I like it. I believe I'd rather my doctor be in charge."

"Ma'am, that's over. We'll just have to adapt the best we can."

"How soon do you need it?"

"Not a big rush, but sometime in the next month. I'm gonna set up a meeting with Chick Crawley and I'll need it before that."

She checked her calendar. "It'll take about three days."

"No problem. I'm an open book. Come make yourself at home. Just sign one of the HIPAA forms with Peg and go at it."

The evaluation was ready after three days of pencil-pushing. "Can you meet tomorrow, Doc?" Fountain asked.

"Sure. I'll try to block off a full hour. Lunch okay? I can have Peg bring in something from the B and B."

"Fine. Will your other doctors be there?"

"Nah. Dee had to go check on his mama and Lucas has to do some gymnastics physicals at school. I'll bring 'em up to speed."

"Fine."

They met in the breakroom, and Fountain lay out the spreadsheets. "These things are complicated, Bones. Everyone looks at the acquisition price, but you also have to view it in context of real estate evaluation and also the ongoing employment contractual arrangements."

"Try telling that to Riley Harper."

She raised an eyebrow, and pulled out some more papers. "Let's see, I believe you own the real estate, correct?"

"Yes, ma'am. I rent it to the others. I might add I always set the rent kinda low. They were good to me, and I never wanted to give them any incentive to consider other space."

She shook her head. "You aren't a business guy at all, huh?"

"Nope. I'm a doctor guy, not a money guy. But you know what they call docs who mistreat their partners: Solo practitioners." Bones went to get some coffee. "I'm proud to say I've had the same wife, the same partners, and the same nurses all these years. Loyalty ought to be worth something."

She smiled. "I'm afraid you're antiquated, at least if you're gonna deal with Raleigh."

"Maybe so." Bones poured up some coffee. "Care for a cup?"

"Thanks." She put the real estate appraisal on the table and sipped her coffee. "So what did they offer on your building?"

"They never would tell me."

She set her coffee down. "Wouldn't tell you? How did they expect you to decide if it was fair?"

"Beats me."

She shook her head. "I'm gonna go over this in detail, Bones, but I gotta tell you if they don't get close to this, I'd hire a negotiator. They are trained in this business. You're taught things like empathy and compassion; worthless commodities in the business end of your job. They'll beat you every way they can."

"I'm beginning to understand. We've talked to Charles Thombley out of Atlanta."

"Good. He's excellent."

"So what kind of numbers do you have?" Bones asked.

"Well, on the positive side, you guys are busy. But your fees are too low, and you have some bad debt."

"A lot of 'em can't afford to go to the doctor. These are hard times."

"I assure you the Raleigh boys don't care about that." She flipped to the back page. "My best estimate, give or take a three percent margin of error, is in the range of a half million."

Bones laughed out loud.

Fountain scratched her head. "I realize it's not much. If this were a hardware store, it'd be worth three times as much, a plumber maybe more, but this is a doctor's office. I didn't mean to insult you."

"Insult me? No, ma'am. You don't understand. That's near ten times what Riley Harper quoted. He said sixty-three grand was the max Stark law would allow."

"Sixty-three thousand? Good Lord, Bones. I've heard of being low-balled, but that's crazy. You have two partners."

"Yes, ma'am, and we will have a fourth partner after Billy's first year."

"Even though he's not a partner yet his employment does figure into the appraisal. The practice is more valuable with another doctor," she said.

Bones sighed. "You know, Ms. Fountain, Harper didn't take our young Dr. Spurgeon into account at all. In bluegrass we always say a man who will steal from you with a fountain pen is just as dangerous as one who'd steal from you with a pistol."

"'Tis sad, but true. I see it all the time in my line of work," she replied.

"Billy Spurgeon could make a lot more money anywhere besides Harvey County. He'll stay if we can generate some semblance of stability, but I can't sell for what Riley Harper opened with and offer Billy a competitive salary while we wait to see how the arrangement works out. Heck, the three of us docs, Billy, and a PA would all work ourselves half to death for what they pay Riley Harper every year to rip people off. He's a rascal."

"We live in a strange world, Bones. Let me be sure you understand my recommendations as to the ongoing employment contracts for the docs."

"Yes, ma'am."

"And when do you meet with Chick?"

"Mr. Thombley had me put it off for a month."

She spread out the papers. "You've got time, then. You might have a chance; Chick is a reasonable man. I heard he saved the day with Dr. Greene's practice."

"Really?"

"Yep." She opened the document. "So, look here at line twelve on page seven. You gotta have a clause like this or they'll just take it out of your income over time."

"Yes, ma'am."

"Now, see this phrase? I want you to be ready—"

Peg brought in lunch.

"Let's take a minute to eat, Ms. Fountain. I've got a notion I might be sick later," Bones said.

"You need a Co-Cola, Doc?" Peg asked.

"I'm afraid so. Do we still have her Uncle Pete's song in the office CD player?"

"Just 'A Closer Walk'?"

"Yes, ma'am. How 'bout putting it on? I'm gonna need all the help I can get."

"Sure, Doc. Whatever song you need." Peg went to put on the music.

Chapter Eighteen

Chick called one morning. "Doc, when are we gonna meet?"

"It might be about a month, Chick. I've kinda got a full plate right now."

"No problem. Man, it's gonna be up to me and you to save the family farm. I've met with Riley Harper. He doesn't have a clue about life in Harvey County."

"So what's wrong with that cat, Chick? Doesn't he realize what we do for the hospital?"

"He should. You've been the number one producer for a quarter century and the others are in the top five. They'd just like to squeeze some more outta ya."

"Man, it ain't just the money they make off me. It's the little things, too. Remember when old lady Hamlet was post-op and gonna sue 'cause she was mad over her pain medicine?"

"Yeah, the surgeons got tired of all that bitching and wouldn't hear any more of it after a while."

"In a way, you can hardly blame 'em," Bones replied. "She's mean as all get out. It wasn't even my case and I went up there and smoothed it over."

"The family didn't have a case. We'd have won in court."

"That's true, but don't forget how much time and trouble I saved you guys. One 'How can I help you, ma'am?' is better than a thousand 'I'm gonna kick your asses.'"

Chick laughed. "I do remember, and I appreciate it, too. You have to realize the folks who run this business nowadays don't have anything to do with patients. This is a money game. Sick people are just an aggravation. When I first got into heath care all we talked about was germs. Now all we talk about is money."

Bones rubbed his chin. "When I started our patients were the only reason to be. Now you can barely see 'em for all the paperwork."

"You are so old-fashioned."

"Yeah, well, now it's almost like 'Something has to be done about all these patients; they're getting in the way of my paperwork.'" Bones sighed. "It is frustrating, but I gotta stay in business. I hope you and I can work it out. You's my people, Chick. Riley Harper . . . . Well, I hate to talk bad about anybody but I don't think he's one of us."

"I agree, but don't say I said it."

"Promise."

They no more than got off the phone and Peg beeped Bones. "There's a Mr. Chevalier on line two. Is that someone you know?"

"Hm. Not really, but he's the CEO at Sandhills. Yeah, put him on."

"Mr. Chevalier? This is Dr. James Robertson, How can I help you?"

"Aren't you the doctor who plays music?" he asked.

"Yes, sir. That's me."

"You would have enjoyed this weekend. I was at the old alma mater for the induction of the first female president at Harvard, and one of your kind of people was there."

"Really? Who was that?"

"Uh, I forgot the name. She was a banjo player."

"Really? What did she look like?"

"Young, blond, looked like some kind of California surfer girl."

"Oh, that had to be Alison Brown. She and her husband Garry West own Compass Records in Nashville, Tennessee."

"I didn't know people played the banjo like that. I love jazz, and I could hear some of that in her playing."

"You have a good ear, friend. She can play Scruggs style with the best of 'em, but is also one of the premier jazz banjoists in the country. Besides, bluegrass ain't nothing but hillbilly jazz, anyway."

"Interesting. Well, she was excellent."

"No doubt. Hey, she's one of your people, too, sir."

"How's that?" Chevalier asked.

"You know why they invited her?"

"I assume for that spectacular music."

"Sure, that's part of it. But it is also because she has an MBA from your alma mater just like you do."

"Really?"

"Yes, sir. And also it is because she and her husband run a very successful business, Compass Records. They have the best selection going, not only in bluegrass, but old time, Celtic, and your jazz, too. Compass will point you in the right direction. Check 'em out."

"I will. Bones, you need to come visit us sometime. I've heard you do some community medicine preceptorships for us and we appreciate it. We're only an hour from the beach. It's pretty country; we have great seafood. Come visit."

"I will, sir." Bones looked at his watch. "I guess I better split. My first patient is ready."

"Very well. Have a good day."

"Yes, sir."

Chapter Nineteen

As he got older, Bones began to take after Indie in many ways. Back when Indie was on his death bed, he'd laugh, and say, "Bones you're morphing."

"Whaddaya mean, Indie?"

"Morphing. You're turning into me. It's a sure sign my time on earth is near the end."

Bones would get out of his chair and walk over to the bedside, then pull up Indie's covers and tuck him in a bit. "Hush, Indie. You're just cold; getting some kinda delirium or something. Don't say such as that."

"It's true." Indie coughed. "Hell, you ain't got a frivolous bone in ya and I don't have a delirious one. I've spent my whole adult life trying to get you not to worry so much."

Bones smiled. "Well, you got to admit you've helped me some."

"Some? Boy, you're the only student I ever had who made an A in both medicine and bluegrass." He coughed harder and grabbed his chest. "I'm like the old lion in *The Lion King*. There ain't nothing left I can pass on to you."

Bones would jump up and all but shout. "Yeah, there is, Indie. Don't you talk like that. You're the best there ever was. I learn something every time I talk to you."

"Now it is up to you to carry on."

Bones wiped his eyes. "I ain't as good as you, Indie."

"You're even better, boy."

"No way."

"By the way, don't take up cigarettes, young'un. Bad habit."

"Yes, sir." Bones would bite his fingernails as he promised.

Bones thought of Indie as he placed the call. "Chick, we need to play golf. I gotta talk to you about this acquisition. I'm ready to set a time to meet. We need to get something settled. Billy's doing good, but I need to be able to tell him what direction we're headed in. You wouldn't believe the offers these kids get nowadays. He's gonna make partner before you know it, and Harvey County doesn't need to have him lured away."

"When can you meet? Is two Wednesdays from now over lunch okay?"

"Sure, okay."

"You want to get in a round of golf at River Run this Wednesday?"

"Sure. See you then. Call me a tee time."

"Will do." After he hung up Bones called Mr. Thombley to be sure he could make the meeting in two weeks. Thombley had a meeting close by that day in the morning so they were on.

Chick and Bones teed it up at River Run the next Wednesday. Neither were pros, but both were accomplished players. They teed up without any negotiations.

"I'm not much in a gambling mood today," Bones said.

"Me, neither. Not good to play poker with you, anyway. We'll get a hot dog at the turn. I'll put it on the hospital tab."

"Okay."

Bones brought it up first. "Chick, I'm just like Indie about the fall of the year. It gives me a touch of the blues, too. Winter's coming on. I really don't care for change, but I have to adapt to what is. I'd like to make the change as palatable as possible, and don't want to hurt too many people in the process."

"I'm for that, too."

"I can see I'm not gonna be able to make this happen alone. I had to hire a negotiator."

"I understand. Who'd ya get?"

"Charles Thombley."

Chick grunted and did not respond further.

"Okay, man. I know he can be a hardball player, but I'm the boss. I guess it's a strange way to negotiate, but I'm up front. I want to stay on the home team if they'll just let me. I can't give it away, though, you know that."

"Thombley's tough. Riley Harper's gonna hate him."

"That's probably a good sign for me. I know he's tough, but I've already told him you guys are my friends and I'm not gonna go elsewhere unless forced to. I'm not gonna strong arm you, either. I want you and Thombley to negotiate out what's fair. If you do, I'll shake hands on it, and Riley Harper will have to live with it."

"You realize this puts me in jeopardy."

"I do, Chick. If a deal doesn't work out when it comes time to lay blame you can count on it that they'll put it on you. You can also count on the fact that I'll defend you."

"I'm sure you will, Bones, but nobody's gonna listen to a country doctor."

Bones laughed. "Gotta hand it to you, Chick. At least you're honest. I know they don't pay any attention to me now. There's only one problem, though. As long as I'm around I'll have the leverage that comes with the truth, and will be able to hold the disingenuous at bay. It's like what Indie did with Betty in our Mandolin Case; had her in a spot where she couldn't do him wrong because it'd hurt her more than anyone. I hope the dang fools don't put me in that position, but if they do, so be it."

"God Almighty, you're an obsessive little SOB."

"That's what Indie used to say."

They putted out on number nine. Chick handed Bones the scorecard. "We're slick. Let's go get a hot dog."

"Okay."

Chapter Twenty

Bones wanted to meet with Charles Thombley out of town. He placed the call. "I'm gonna be in Charlotte at the end of the month cause Tim O'Brien is over at Spirit Square. Any chance we can meet?"

"Sure. I've got some business over that way with Carolinas Medical Center."

"Good. Most of the medical people over there don't know me. I'd rather stay under the radar as much as I can for now. We won't have any eavesdroppers over that way. Where do you want to meet?"

"How 'bout the Open Kitchen?"

"Over near the stadium?" Bones asked.

"That'd be fine," Charles relied.

"Cool. What time?"

"Six-thirty. I'd like to finish up in time to see Tim O'Brien, too."

"Good."

They checked out the menu. Bones ordered lasagna, and Thombley went for a small Mama K special pizza and a Greek salad. Bones handed the menu back to the waitress.

"I'd like plenty of that good sweet tea. My cousin lives in Gastonia and comes over here every few weeks. He says it's the best."

"Yes, sir. Since nineteen fifty-two." She went to place their orders.

"So what's your take on the deal?" Bones asked.

"Thombley sipped on his water. "Chick knows you can't sign it. Even Marvin does but he can't admit it openly."

"Are they willing to move any at all?"

"No question. They both know if they fail to do so, there are other places you can look. No one at Harvey Memorial wants that. CMA doesn't either, but my guess is Riley Harper thinks you're bluffing. I talked to Chick a long time Wednesday. He's willing to deal and Marvin has granted him some latitude. More important, he knows he'd better; there's a lot to lose here."

"You know Chick saved the Greene practice, and about lost his job."

"Yeah, we talked about that. Chick's in a tough spot. They all know you guys are close and play golf together. If he doesn't take action and it gets away he'll get the blame, and if he negotiates and keeps you but pays a fair price he'll get the blame for that, too. He can't win. He'll have to at least get it by Stanley. "

"Stanley? I'm telling ya, man, I don't think he'll stand up to Riley Harper, and Riley ain't gonna like this one bit."

"I've dealt with Riley before. He's gonna have to give in on this one."

"We'll see." Bones sighed. "This Harper is a thorn, man."

"I agree."

Bones called Chick the night before the meeting. "Look, pal, I look forward to our meeting. We'll make something work. Of course, now I have Thombley involved. He won't let me sign anything that isn't fair."

"Yeah, I've talked to him some."

"So what's your take on it?"

"Everyone knows Thombley. He's tough."

Bones paused for a minute. "Look, Chick, I ain't trying to be a butt about this thing, but I've got a lot of folks to answer to. You know I can't sign anything like that deal."

"I know."

"I'm not trying to strong arm you either, though. Look, we've worked together a long time. Y'all just get to something fair and I'm gonna stick with the home team."

"I understand."

Bones thought back to Indie. "I suppose it's a crazy kind of negotiation, but all I want is just to be reasonable. If Charles gets too rough, I'll hold him back, but there's no way I'm gonna close the deal alone."

"We won't let him run over us. I can't and keep my job. Don't worry. We'll get a deal cut."

"Okay. I'll see you at the Chick Coop in the morning. I don't know why, but I'm still optimistic. You and I have I have always been able to talk turkey at your office. We've solved a lot of problems at the Coop. I still think we can make this happen, Riley Harper notwithstanding."

"Me, too, Doc."

The three met at Chick's office. After some small talk about golf, Thombley got to the business at hand. Soon he and Chick were engrossed in numbers Bones had little understanding of.

"What does that mean?" Bones asked.

"I'll go over it later," Thombley said. "Look at line five, Chick." Thombley pointed to the document. "He can't agree to that. RVUs are outdated, anyway, at least as a sole measure of physician worth."

"Yes, but we have to have some way to evaluate productivity," Chick said.

"I agree, but . . . ."

Bones nodded off.

"Scratch line seven on page eighteen," Thombley said.

"Okay."

After a few hours the document began to shape up. Thombley lay it to the side. "What do you think, Chick?"

"Fair deal. I'll draw it up for a final review."

All three men shook hands. Bones and Thombley left. Chick went back to his desk to work.

They walked to the parking lot and got in Thombley's Lexus. "So, boss, whaddaya think?" Bones asked.

"It should be a deal. We'll know soon."

"Good."

Chick returned the preliminary documents in a week. "The boss hasn't signed off on 'em, but I've run the numbers. We can make money on it."

"Let us know."

Another week went by. Thombley called. "Looks like we might have a deal."

"Really?" Bones asked.

"Stanley signed off on it. The contract is in the mail."

"Great." Bones tossed his pen in the air and caught it on the way back down. "I wanted to stay on the home team if at all possible."

"It looks like you should be able to."

The contract came in on Friday.

Dr. Dee came by to hear the verdict. Bones began to read through it. "Hey, wait a minute," Bones said. "This isn't what we shook hands on." He slammed his fist on the desk. "Four and a quarter is a bit off top dollar but fair enough. This is the same as far as the purchase price we agreed on, but I don't like the language in the doctor's ongoing contract. Damn it, they're gonna try to extract it out of us over time."

"You sure?" Ed asked.

"Uh, I think so. I better fax this over to Thombley."

In fifteen minutes, Peg stuck her head in the office. "Mr. Thombley is on line one. He says it's urgent."

"Yes, ma'am."

Bones picked up the receiver.

"Don't sign!" Thombley yelled.

"Yes, sir." Bones broke the news to the other docs, and then called Chick. "Damn it, Chick, this ain't what we agreed to."

"Are you sure?"

"Yes."

"It's on my desk; let me get back with you."

Chick called back in ten minutes. "Uh, Bones, well, I'm not sure. This Thombley is a smart guy, and frankly he's more of an expert than I am, and——"

"C'mon, Chick. You know as well as I do this isn't what we shook hands on. Who changed the yearly employment contract?"

"I don't know. I have my suspicions."

"Riley Harper?"

"I dunno."

"Chick, you know I can't sign this."

"I know."

"Let me ask you something. I'm not dealing with anything like the Mafia, am I?"

"Well, no, not that bad. They aren't gonna kill you or anything."

"Why did they change it?"

"Bones, you know I can't be quoted on anything against the home team."

"I understand."

"It's like this, my friend. To them you are only a business machine, a way to make money. That's it. They just tweaked it to make more money. My guess is they suspected you wouldn't even notice."

"Good Lord. Well, I'll be back in touch. You know what this means, don't you?"

"I'm afraid I do."

Chapter Twenty One

Bones tossed and turned all night. In times of trouble he would always write, remembering Flannery O'Conner, who said, "How can I know what I think until I read what I write?" Or Mark Twain, who used to say that when he saw trouble, he'd write his way through it.

Kate always told Bones, "Honey, write it down. Later, if you decide not to use it, and most of the time you will, it can help you think your way out of a jam. Later, if you don't use it right away at least hang onto it for another day, but if you write it down it'll help you gel your thoughts." Bones always thought Kate had good advice and always held it close. He asked her where she came up with the idea and she said she'd gone to a lecture in college by a famous Southern literary agent and she never forgot it.

With the disappointment of a fair deal with friends undermined, Bones began to keep notes with an increased intensity.

Bones e-mailed Thombley early the next morning: Game on. I thought we were in a gentleman's agreement to try to sell our practice to our friends, and at a discount at that. Instead, this is nothing but a giant damn car deal on steroids.

It seems at this point I have no choice but to ask you to seek out all options. Discuss with all interested parties and report back to me. The death of medicine as a healing art and cottage industry is at hand, and the final blow has been dealt for us. I am left no choice but to free you to explore any and all options that might be in our interest.

Thombley returned: They have made a serious error. Will get back to you.

Bones called Chick. "Bud, we're old friends. I feel like I owe it to you to make sure you understand, but from here on, the negotiations are in Charles Thombley's hands. I'm gonna do what he says, period."

"I understand."

"You know if this goes against Raleigh, they're gonna have a scapegoat lined up ahead of time."

"I'm sure you are correct."

"You realize it will be you."

"I'm afraid you're right."

"Chick, you're the ultimate survivor. They have one problem, I know the truth, and you can count on me to tell it. You had a deal cut; it ain't your fault. After it's all over they won't want me to talk, and you'll be safe because of it."

"As an institution, we have made a mistake. I just hope it's not terminal."

"There's still a chance, but now it's competitive."

"Who else is he gonna put on the game?"

"You know the players as well as I do, Chick."

"I guess so."

Bones and Dr. Dee stopped at Chang's Chinese for lunch. "Bluegrass wonton," Bones ordered.

It was a new server. "Bluegrass wonton? So sorry, what is?"

"Bluegrass wonton. Wonton soup with a little white rice tossed in."

"Bluegrass wonton. No one else order, but we will make."

"So, Dee, who all do you think Charles will call on?" Bones asked.

"Sandhills, no doubt. I guess Novell is a possible player, but Winston is pretty far from Harvey County; I'm not sure they have a vested interest in the landscape here. Sandhills has had its eye on Harvey County for years and has already been able to grow market share. We could jump start it big-time, though."

"I agree." Bones sipped his tea. "Man, can you believe how stupid Raleigh is about this? We've been the number one provider for more than two decades at Harvey Memorial and they are treating us like an expendable item. Disgusting."

"It does make you wonder how they'd treat us after we signed. If the dating is this bad, I can't imagine being married to 'em. Yeah, it's unreal. I wish I knew if it were Stanley alone or if the direction came all the way from Raleigh."

'I think it's mostly Raleigh, but it's a little of both. Politically, Stanley can't stand up to Harper and keep his job. Riley Harper has made it clear he won't negotiate with a hillbilly. It's a perfect storm for a failure."

"As Cool Hand Luke's prison captain would say, 'What we have here is a failure to communicate.'" Dr. Dee laughed.

"Yep. 'Acquisition Syndrome Breakdown'; it'd make a good banjo tune."

The server brought their soup. "Bluegrass wonton."

Dee dipped into his wonton. "Riley Harper should know better than to try to cheat a bluegrass man. Most of all you. You're the most stubborn rascal I ever ran into. I'm just glad we're on the same team."

"Me, too, Dee. You're honest. That's what I like about you."

Chapter Twenty Two

One Monday morning when Billy arrived at the office he heard a banjo. The three-finger rolls were recognizable but faltered at times. He followed the music to the front. It led to Dr. Robertson's office. He stuck his head in the door.

"Bones! I had no idea you played the banjo."

"I don't. At least not now. Now at one time I played pretty good. I played the Amphitheatre with SawBones Grass at the Tennessee Worlds' Fair in nineteen eighty-two. We opened for John Hartford. I played "Dear Old Dixie." Bones laughed. "They called me the 'Harvey County Flash.'" He ran over a few bars. "Not exactly a speed demon now. Can't play much of it anymore, at least not fast. We have the annual Hee-Haw show three weeks from Wednesday and no one in the church knows how to play it but me. I only know three chords and the truth, but I've got a capo and some of those little model railroad spikes to hook the fifth string. From one year to the next they forget I play the same licks I played the year before."

"Whatcha gonna do for a mandolin player?" Billy asked.

"I taught my niece a little. She can chop chords." Bones rolled through a new minor chord run he'd learned from Brownie Scott. "How do you like that one?"

"Cool." Billy smiled.

"Will you bring your guitar?" Bones asked.

"Sure, but it's on a Wednesday. I always have call coverage that night."

"No problem. I already talked to Dr. Dee. He'll cover you."

"Great."

Bones played a few bars of "Foggy Mountain Breakdown." "Hey, the gig is still three weeks off. I can get Dr. Dee to play guitar and Lucas to cover call. Why don't you learn the banjo and play the gig for us?"

"Three weeks? Right."

"It can be done." Bones put the banjo in the corner, picked up his mandolin, and raced through "Rawhide." "Years ago our mandolin player left for Nashville, so I bought a mandolin and played the gig."

"In three weeks?"

"Trust me, it wasn't very good. My daughter always said the reason I was able to learn to play the mandolin as an adult was I had no shame. I played a lot of gigs before I had any idea what I was doing, but we kept the music going. All that mattered to me was to keep the music alive; I didn't really care which instrument I played to make that happen. Indie always used to say to be a compassionate doctor you had to have some music in you."

Bones looked at his diploma on the wall. "Right from the get-go we start with a cadaver and as young people we see more heartache and tragedy than what any impressionable soul should ever see. Then we are taught to stuff it all way deep inside and not let it out. Indie always said we had to get shed of all that bad karma somehow or we'd turn cynical, and music is how we did it. For him it was the fiddle; in my case, it was the mandolin. Somehow I've got a notion you're a banjo man. Heck, I'm a banjo guy, too, at least a little bit, but as busy as we are as doctors, it's probably best to concentrate on one instrument."

"Sorta like a major in college."

"Yep. I majored in mandolin with a minor in guitar, bass, and banjo. Man, it's been a bunch of fun and it sure beats drinking to deal with the stress." Bones reached over, picked up the banjo, and handed it to Billy. "Tell ya what, I'll play a few licks in G. You just strum across the open strings on the banjo while I play."

Billy cradled the banjo and brushed across the strings.

"See," Bones said, "nuttin' to it."

Billy grimaced. "I don't think Brownie Scott would call that banjo music."

"Everybody starts at the beginning."

Billy put the banjo across his lap and looked it over. "No name on the peg-head. What kind is it?"

Bones picked it up again and played a couple more rolls. "I'm getting warmed up, young'un. This, my boy, is an original one-of-a-kind Stewart McDonald custom version I put together myself." He hit another run. "Okay, I admit it's no Mastertone, but this very banjo once played the Tennessee Amphitheater. We opened for John Hartford after I'd only been playing a year, and he became a friend anyway." He handed it to Billy. "Take it home."

"Gee, Bones, I hate to take it."

"I want it back someday. After you learn to play you'll want a better one. They call it BAS."

"What's that?"

"Banjo Acquisition Syndrome."

"The things ya gotta do to make partner around here . . . ." Billy grinned.

Bones laughed out loud. "You're hooked." He put the banjo in the case, took it to Billy's office, and walked back up the hall. "Nuff horsing around, kid. I didn't get to be senior partner picking the banjo."

"Nah, you did that with the mandolin."

"You want to know the real secret, Billy?"

"Sure."

"It's the gray hair. All you gotta do is hang around 'til you have the most gray hair. Nuttin' to it." Bones laughed, put his stethoscope around his neck, and picked up the chart in the box on the door to Exam Room One. He motioned for Lynn O'Carroll. "Hey, Lynn, he's doctor by day and banjo man by night; Banjo Billy's gonna make partner in six months, just wait and see."

Lynn nodded. "I have no doubt."

Chapter Twenty Three

Back when he was alive, Indie did some things few people knew about. When he'd read a journal article he liked, he'd write a letter to the doctors who published it, and tell them all about Harvey County and what a fine place it was to live.

Some of them went unread, but most of the time he'd get back a thank you note. Indie always said he might write a hundred to find one, but someday some doctor would show up who wanted to look into small town life.

Several years after Indie died, a man showed up at Harvey Memorial. He had grown weary of the politics of big institutions, and wanted to consider a simpler lifestyle. He'd kept Indie's letter all those years, and came to look around. Bones had to laugh. Indie'd been in the grave five years, and here he was still showing folks Harvey County. After two visits, Grinzler Zelnorm bought a farm outside of town and set up shop.

Bones took to Grinz right away. Harvey County had never had a GI specialist, and this one was from the Mayo

Clinic, no less. Until Grinz arrived, Bones had been Harvey County's ace bubble test-taker. Bones was smart, but Grinz was brilliant. Bones wasn't jealous, saw the opportunity, and made friends with Grinz as soon as he hit town.

"I always want to hang out with the best, brother. Never know what you might learn. I'm so glad to meet you." Bones shook his hand. "Man, am I gonna keep you busy. If I never look up anyone's rear end again it'll suit me just fine." Bones retired his sigmoidoscope that very day.

One day, Grinz wanted to show Bones an x-ray. "Whaddaya think that is, pal?"

"Looks like a little camera to me."

"Correct. Why do you think it's there?"

"Stuck, I reckon."

"Damn, you're good. The medical center sent her back to me undiagnosed. I told 'em their fancy high-tech had made the diagnosis for me. Drew an X on her belly with an arrow that said CUT HERE. Pissed 'em off good."

"What did they do?"

"What could they do? The lady had an acute abdomen from their camera; they had to operate."

"What did they find?"

"The camera was stuck in a carcinoid tumor. I asked 'em to send it to me as a memento, but I never got it."

Bones laughed. "Indie would be proud."

Grinz motioned Bones off to the side. "Heard you might sell."

"Where'd ya hear that?"

"Been playing pool with Snook. Don't worry. I'm all for you, and I'm discreet, too. Man, after years of swimming in the Mayo shark waters, I might have a few pointers."

"Cool. When can we meet?"

"I like breakfast."

"Good. The B and B okay?"

"Sure."

"Friday?"

"Got it."

Chapter Twenty Four

Before Rose came along, the phones were often a worry for Harvey Family. They had one lady who was excellent but after she retired they wondered if there'd ever be another one that good. All those worries went away when Peg and Lynn O'Carroll found Rose and recommended her. Some of the non-clinical personnel wanted to have too much authority and liked to try to give medical advice, and some would rather read *Cosmopolitan* than pick up the line. Bones was a laid-back kind of guy, but if an employee didn't put the patient first he could turn on a dime. He'd fired more than one over the issue.

It all changed with Rose, though. Once he hired her, he never looked back, and any new employees had to meet her standard. Bones was never one for extensive employee manuals and had few rules. When they'd ask how to handle the telephones, Bones would say, "Look, kid, just do like Rose. If you aren't sure what to do, ask her, then follow her advice."

Rose was one of the few who could handle Rick Lester, the local Chrysler dealer.

Lester had once called and demanded Bones complete a form so he could swim at the Y.

Rose came to ask Dr. Bones.

"Last time I saw him his blood pressure was up. I don't know whether he's safe to swim or not. Tell him he'll have to come in," Bones said.

Rose went back to the phone to explain. Lester was insistent. "You tell Bones I don't appreciate him wasting my time. I'm a busy man."

Rose relayed the message to Bones. "He doesn't think he can come in right now."

Bones stopped reading the chart and pulled his stethoscope off his neck. "He never wants to come in. Tell him I can't certify he's safe without an exam. For all I know he has heart disease nowadays. Tell him no tickee, no washee."

"Yes, sir." Rose went back to her station. "Mr. Lester? Yes, he said he is so sorry he has to trouble you, but the State Board has their regulations, you know. I'm so sorry. Can I book you on a Tuesday? I know it's a little lighter at the car lot that day, and Jimmy comes in early to help you."

"Okay. Damn. Okay. That Board is just interested in doctors' getting my money."

Rose sighed. "I'm sorry, sir; we'll take good care of you."

Lester made the appointment but again complained when he got there.

Bones washed his hands. "Look, friend. Don't you understand what this form is for?"

"Sure. It's so I can swim at the Y."

"No, it ain't, brother. It's in case you drown in the pool, everyone will know who they are supposed to sue."

Lester flunked the treadmill test Bones ordered, had bypass surgery, and still grumbled about the inconvenience.

So on this Wednesday morning three years later, Rose already knew the man's temperament.

"Rose, this is Rick Lester. Tell Bones to call me in something for a headache; I've got me a humdinger."

"Dr. Robertson is off today. Dr. Spurgeon has an opening."

"Then tell Billy to call it in."

"Now, Mr. Smith, you know Billy can't call in something for a headache without checking you. We'd be glad to work you in this morning."

"Damn it, Rose. I'm a busy man. I ain't got time to come over there. You tell Billy it's the third week of the month and we ain't made the nut factor yet. He'll know what I'm talking about."

Rose found Billy in the hall at room five with a chart. Billy heard out the story.

"For all I know he might have an aneurysm. I'll be glad to see him, but I can't diagnose him without an exam. What is it Bones says? Diagnose first; treat later. No tickee, no washee."

"Yes, sir. By the way, what is the nut factor?" Rose asked.

"Huh? Oh, that's the break-even point. It's when they've sold enough cars to know they will clear expenses for the month. The car biz is enough to drive you nuts."

"Like the doctor business?" Rose asked.

"Yes, ma'am, I guess so."

Lester wasn't happy about it, but agreed to an appointment. "It'll have to be this afternoon, though. I've got too much on tap for the morning."

"Okay, We've got you booked at three-thirty. Make sure you bring in all your medicines."

"Hell, Billy knows what I'm taking. He and Bones write all of 'em. They ought to know what they prescribe."

"Yes, sir, but bring them anyway. He likes to look at them each time." Rose went on to another call.

By 3:30, Billy was already behind, but saw Lester at 4:00. "Damn it, Spurgeon, my time is just as valuable as yours. I don't appreciate you being late."

"Yes, sir. I apologize." Billy had already given up explanations. "When did your headache start?"

"This SOB's been going on for two weeks. I was over at the ER Friday night and what they gave me ain't worth a damn. Something's gotta be done." Lester grew quieter. "This thing's bad, Billy, I tell you. Been waking me up in the middle of the night."

Uh, oh. Middle of the night. Red flag there, Billy thought.

"Can't you just give me a shot and knock it out? I've got a lot to do this month."

Billy smiled. *Diagnose first, treat later.* He looked over the intake sheet. "What did they give you in the ER? Did you bring your medicines?"

"Nah, but I told the nurse what they were. Didn't you get that from the ER?"

Rose tracked down the fax.

Fiorocet, hm. Barbiturate. Billy's wheels began to turn. "Mr. Lester, are you still taking Coumadin; you know, rat poison?"

"Yeah, yeah, ever since that clot on my lungs last spring."

"Did you ever see the specialist?"

"Nah, hell no. You're doing okay with it. Yeah, them SOBs wanted me over there every month and the co-pay is too high. It's cheaper to see you. I wasn't gonna do that."

"Have you had your blood checked?"

"I think the VA did it."

"When?"

"I dunno."

Billy started down the routine checklist. Most of it was negative but when he asked about the kidneys there were some clues.

"Any burning when you pee? Prostate problems? Anything like that?"

Lester looked at his watch. "Come to think of it, yeah, I was at the VA a couple weeks ago when my prostate flared up."

"What did they give you?"

"I don't know; a great big pill."

"Was it twice a day? Maybe with a real long name, something like Trimethoprim Sulfamethoxazole?"

"Nah, just a bunch of letters. SMZTMP, something like that."

Damn, Billy thought. *Sulfa. One of those things every third-year med student ought to know. Sulfa and Coumadin don't mix. Barbiturate, too. It was a standard Board question from way back.*

Billy proceeded to the exam; there were no neurological findings. "Mr. Lester, let me check your blood. I'll be back in a minute."

"Last time you said that it was a half hour."

"I'll be right back. Just hang on."

Chapter Twenty Five

Billy checked the lab report. INR – 5. *Dang it.* He went back to talk to Lester.

Billy sat down and lay the report on the exam table. "Man, your blood is way too thin."

"The VA said it was okay."

"Yeah, but that was before the sulfa. Have you hit your head?"

"Don't think so." Lester stroked his chin. "Hey, wait a minute. I was out on my sailboat a couple weeks ago and the boom whacked me."

"Did it knock you out?"

"Nah. Didn't think much about it."

"You ever had a headache like this before?"

"Nope."

Billy checked Lester's strength and reflexes again. "Normal." He stood up. "You need a CT scan."

"You sure?" Lester chewed his fingernails.

"Yep. Might have a subdural, which is a blood clot on your brain."

Billy went to work to get approval. The insurance company didn't agree. He called Bones at home to relay the story.

"Who's the chart jockey for the insurance company?" Bones asked.

"Some guy named Robbins."

"You tell that SOB if he delays the diagnosis, Martin Taylor, the attorney, waits in the wings for a class-action lawsuit and I'll do anything I can to help him."

Billy got permission. He wanted it that night but by then it was after six and Radiology wouldn't schedule it until later. He went back to Lester. "They said they'd catch you at nine tonight or first thing in the a.m."

"Ah, tell 'em to go to hell. I'll get it in the morning. I ain't gonna wait around that long tonight."

"If you get worse, you better go to the ER. I'd rather you did it tonight."

"Whatever."

The next morning was a full schedule. Billy realized at eleven that he hadn't gotten his call report. "Lynn, better get hold of that report."

Several phone calls and two hours later the call came in from Dr. Powers. "Billy? Are you looking for a subdural on Lester?"

"Yep."

"Good diagnosis, kid. It's not too big and he doesn't have any shift. It might resolve without surgery."

"Good Lord. We gotta find him."

Billy called Lester's car lot and got Jim, the Used Car manager. "Nah, man," Jim said. "The boss went home at lunch. Ain't been back."

"Was he okay?"

"Said he felt better."

Billy knew one of the nurses, Lynn O'Carroll, went to church with Lester's wife, so he had her make the call. "Julie? We need to get Rick back over here to the office. Is he there?"

"Something wrong?"

"He might need some surgery."

"My goodness. He was feeling better and went down to Morehead to check on his boat."

When O'Carroll reported to Billy, he slammed the chart on his desk. "The beach?" *That guy is so hard-headed I don't know how he got a subdural anyway.* "We gotta find him."

Lester's cell didn't work. It was a long afternoon. "I hope he's okay." Billy worried out-loud. "Tell his wife to try to find him."

The next day Billy got a call from Carteret County Hospital ER. "Dr. Spurgeon?"

"Yes."

"We're air-lifting a Rick Lester to Sandhills U. Dr. Lee Stuart is already on standby. Lester collapsed on the beach this morning."

"Subdural, right?"

"Yes."

"We've been looking for him. Send me the paperwork." Billy hung up the phone. "Dang it."

Chapter Twenty Six

Brownie Scott might look like a kid, but the woman is an expert on the subject of five-string banjos. When Billy came to ask Bones for an opinion, he did not need to do a background check.

"Doc," Billy asked, "Brownie Scott offered to stop in off the road and give me some banjo lessons here at lunch. Is that okay with office policy?"

"Absolutely. That is great, Billy, you're gonna get lessons from one of the true living masters of the instrument. She's not only a great player, but a woman of integrity, and one of the few young beautiful women we'd allow behind closed doors with a doctor in his office. And she is one of the finest on the five-string banjo in the world. She'll help you a ton, and I'd prefer you be a player by the time you make partner and that ain't far off. Tell you what: I'll tell Peg to cut a check from the practice for the lessons. I think all the partners would agree: We want all our docs involved in the arts. It seems they just don't wind up as cynical in the long run."

"Great. She'll be here next week."

Brownie showed up with an extra banjo in hand. "That little homemade ax you have is fine, Billy, but you need another one to take it to the next level."

"Whatcha got?"

"RB-3, late 'eighties model; not vintage, but a good, pro-quality utility instrument."

"Where'd it come from?"

"You know of the Kentucky Derby Kid?"

"Know of her, haven't met her."

"She has connections at Sandhills. This belonged to an x-ray tech who toured with Larry Cordle, but the boy is off the road now; went back to his day job. He said he'd sell it for eighteen hundred, a bargain in my opinion. KDK said I could hold onto it while I was giving lessons. Said the world needed more bluegrass doctors and for you to play it for a while."

She handed it to Billy and he sighted the neck. "Very nice."

Brownie went on. "Hey, speaking of The Kentucky Derby Kid, the message from her is this: The code word is Real Quiet."

"So we hear. Will stay on the listen out."

"By the way, that Riley Harper has acquired several fakes he might run by you. Beware."

"No problem."

"The whole bluegrass world was suspicious of him in that Simon Crutchfield affair. We have a long memory. I'm like Bones. I have no trust in anything Harper says." Brownie scowled.

"From what I've heard so far, I agree." Billy said.

"Okay, let me hear what you worked up on 'Little Cabin Home' on your own."

Billy stumbled at first but soon began to play a smooth rendition. He closed with a blues lick Bones had shown him, one that Bones had learned from Brownie himself.

"Okay, good, but that is a bit too hot an ending for that tune. That lick belongs in something more like 'In the Gravel Yard.'" She subbed a more pastoral passage to close. "I know men like to play aggressive, but there is a time to play soft, and as a banjo player who is also a mama, this one fits the home theme much better."

Billy smiled. "Old Bones is a smart man. He has always said that when he was coming up, bluegrass was more of a boy's club and we sure are better off now that the ladies are more involved. He says every band is better with at least one female voice. And I agree with him. I learn something from Bones every day. Thanks for the lesson."

"Just make sure I get to come when you make partner. I hear there's always a party. I want to play one with you to celebrate."

"Yes, ma'am."

"I'll be back next month for another lesson. We have a gig in Kinston then."

"Okay." Billy handed her a check. "The practice is paying for the lessons. Bones said it was a good investment in the future and the other doctors agreed."

Chapter Twenty Seven

Bones walked by Billy's office the next day and spotted the Gibson logo on the case. "Hey, Banjo Billy, moving up, are ya?"

"Yeah, Doc. It's on loan from Brownie Scott." Billy opened the case, got the banjo out, played a few rolls, and handed it to Bones.

"Very nice," Bones said. "How was the lesson?"

"She knows a lot of banjo. For that matter, she's clued in on a lot of other matters, too."

"Such as?" Bones asked.

"She's met the Kentucky Derby Kid. KDK is well connected at Sandhills. Brownie knew the code word was 'Real Quiet.' She also knew Riley Harper was likely to throw a few more curve balls at us."

"Yeah, Brownie's kept her ear to the ground for us. Musicians know the street just like docs do. If they're gonna survive they have to learn who's who pretty quick. Soon they know which promoter's checks bounce and which record company's royalty statements don't add up right, all that sort of thing. But they love what they do and they persist. One time I heard a fan say they didn't think it was fair those music people got paid for having fun. I told 'em, "Oh, they play for the music for free. It's all the other mess they have to deal with before they ever get on the stage that you pay 'em for: travel, gas, insurance, overhead, time away from home, etc., etc. I'm not sure the fan understood, but they did listen to what I had to say." Bones picked up the banjo and played a few licks. "It's like us. I love being a doc, but having to deal with the Riley Harpers of the world would take the fun out of it if you'd let it." Bones looked at his watch. "I better get started seeing 'em. See ya around lunch."

"Okay, boss." Billy put the banjo in the case and slid it under his desk for the day.

Chapter Twenty Eight

Charles Thombley called with his marching orders. "Okay, Bones, I've rounded up all the usual suspects."

"And the players are?"

"I've considered all your options carefully. Sandhills is your best bet. They already have Harvey County on their long-term strategic plan. They thought it would take a decade but believe the acquisition of Harvey Family could reduce the time commitment goal by a solid fifty percent."

"Any others?"

"Even though Novell is in Winston, they have interest, too."

"What did you tell them?"

"I explained you only went out on one date at a time and liked to explore what any commitment might mean in full before you launched out on another one. I warned them all, though; you might look country, but do not be fooled. If you try to Snooker him, this cat has an army of supporters who will rise to his defense."

"Good. Where is the rendezvous?"

"Don's Italian."

"Got it. You coming?"

"I want you to go alone the first time. I told Chevalier and Sandhills wouldn't be able to understand what all you say, 'cause some would be in bluegrass code, but they best take good notes, and then leave the translation of code into numbers to me and not try to mess with your head; that you planned to leave all the negotiation to me, and that this was just a get-to-know-you meeting anyway. Chevalier said he'd talked to you a little about banjos a month or so ago."

"Charlie, we are a great team. It's 'cause of that head of hair of yours. It's as good as Del McCoury's." Bones thought back to the phone call. "Yeah, I remember that call from Chevalier. I've never had one of those big shots call me about anything, so I was quite surprised."

"Did he hint around about the acquisition at all?"

"Nope. He'd been to the inauguration of the first female president of Harvard and Alison Brown was the entertainment."

"What's he think?"

"He dug it. Liked the jazz influence. I think he was a bit surprised. I told him when I was coming along, banjo players were all old guys who wore coveralls and CAT hats and chewed tobacco; no longer true."

"I'm certain his call was no accident. The man's history is that he does his homework and knows the medical turf in eastern NC. I promise he knows the music is important to you. It's his way of saying he validates you and hopes something works out. He knows the landscape well. He knew you'd show up one day even before you did."

"Well, he sure is off to a better start than Riley Harper. That guy doesn't seem to believe in anything I stand for."

"Harper believes in money. That's it. Period. So how much background do you know about Sandhills? You were in an early class there right?"

"Yes sir. And Billy trained there, of course. I remember the years before the school started. The I-85 'money/power corridor' from Charlotte to Raleigh opposed it fiercely. I guess they were afraid it was gonna steal some of their thunder. Visionary guys like Ed Monroe and Leo Jenkins beat the drum at Rotary and Kiwanis clubs all over the state, not to mention the state legislature. This was before the days of high-priced lobbyists; they just believed in the cause. The message began to take hold. I recall a forward-thinking state legislator, who was also a dentist and a small businessman from Western NC, who began to realize this wasn't just good for eastern NC, it was good for the whole state. Heck, it ended up being good for the entire southeast; Sandhills has got national recognition now as a leader in the development of primary care physicians. When they created the Family Practice Department they didn't tap some cronies from academia, either. Instead they hired a Board Certified Family doctor from the real world, a man who had been in private practice in a little costal North Carolina town. The cat was a tall, young, good-looking man; he had high cheekbones, dark hair and eyes, musta been of Native American ancestry. Man, if you didn't want to be a general practitioner when you got there, you did after a rotation with this guy; he had a million great stories about life as a doctor in the real world. I don't know how they got in the acquisition business."

"Necessity is the mother of invention. Their primary doctors began to face the same pressures you guys have. Some of the practices were outposts for community medicine rotations and many were their very own graduates. They got into it more from a co-operative effort to survive and not so much from an entrepreneurial perspective. Given you and Billy are both graduates they've taken extra interest. Loyalty means something to them. My guess is they'll approach in a kinder and gentler manner than what you have experienced so far."

"Cool. I don't see how it could be any worse," Bones replied.

Sandhills CEO Chevalier and his VP, Royce Ruby, rode to the meeting in the boss's Lexus.

"So how did this guy know about Don's Italian? It's not exactly on most doctor's radar," Ruby asked.

"Either he is an insider or views himself as some kinda populist." Chevalier turned onto Garrison Street. "Doesn't matter, I guess. It's the best Italian in town, and most of the socialites don't frequent it. I hear he likes to send messages. He's got that Charlie Thombley on his team. The guy might not be a businessman, but he has Charles Thombley doing his bidding. We'll have to listen."

"I agree."

They pulled into the parking lot.

"See that truck?" Chevalier asked. "That's his."

"Good God. Is this some kinda MacArthur act? Is this guy real?"

"I hear he is."

Bones had taken the chair at the corner table that faced the exit.

Chevalier and Ruby walked in. Bones stood up as they walked over and extended his hand.

"What's good here, guys?" Chevalier asked.

Don walked over and brushed off the table with a cloth. "No bad here. Ask Dr. Bones. He tell you."

Bones laughed. "Okay, Don. I agree."

They all took a seat at the table. "How's your golf game?" Chevalier asked.

"Seven. Not bad. And you?"

"Off my game."

"That's not what Snook says," Bones replied. "He says you play good for a rich man."

Chevalier raised an eyebrow. "Okay. Six."

Don brought the menus. "Only the best for Dr. Bones, guys. He saved my mama's life when I lived in Harvey County, and—"

Bones held up his hand. "Don, it's okay. They're okay. They're okay."

Don looked over at Ruby. "I believe I see you here before."

"Yes."

"Good. What you like?"

"The marsala, please."

"And you, sir?" Don turned to Chevalier.

"The same."

"And, Doctor, your usual?"

"Sure Don, that's fine."

"Spaghetti and meat balls." Don gathered the menus. "Dr. Bones he never change."

"So we hear," Ruby mumbled. "So how's everything at Harvey Memorial?" he asked Bones.

"Same ol', same ol'," Bones replied. "Slow to join the modern world sometimes, but okay. Change comes slow."

"We hear you are slow to change," Ruby said.

Don brought their drinks.

"Yes sir, I can be, but then again, I don't like to be the last one to catch on either."

"Like the army?" Chevalier asked.

"Yep. Snook was in the army."

"I understand," Chevalier added. "I learned to fly at Fort Rucker."

Don brought their plates and they talked helicopters for a while. Bones wanted to get to the point. He remembered Thrombley's advice: *Don't forget, Doc. This is just a get-to-know-you meeting. Please don't play all your cards on the first visit.* Bones made a silent promise to his pal: *Got it.* Bones sipped on his coffee and considered his opening statement. "Well, guys, I'm a country doctor. I don't know a thing about business, but I believe in getting right to the point. Harvey Memorial, at least through CMA, has been screwing around with this thing for a year and they haven't given me a straight answer yet. We have a big practice, a wonderful staff, and we know our patients. If y'all have looked over all those fancy charts and graphs you've got in your War Room down there at Sandhills, and have some interest in an increased presence and market share in Harvey County, we'd love to talk to you. If you don't, that's okay, and there'd be no hard feelings, but if that's the case I'd rather you not waste my time or yours, and let's just eat this meal and go home."

Chevalier reached over and picked up the check and handed it to Ruby. "Harvey County has been in our strategic plan a long time. As I'm sure you know, we have increased our market share every year. The last five have been especially productive. We'll have our people talk to your people."

"Yes, sir," Bones replied. He handed Mr. Chevalier a card. "My man's name is Charles Thombley." Bones finished his coffee. "I don't know a thing about business. All I know is heart attacks and belly aches. I know a little bluegrass, but no business, and not much golf."

"That's not what Snookers Molesby says." Chevalier laughed.

"I wouldn't pay much attention to Snookers, sir. He's a hustler."

"I won't forget."

Bones called Charles on the way home. "Hey, Del. Met 'em today."

"How'd it go?" he asked.

"Fine, boss. I did just what you said. It was just a get-to-know-you meeting. I gave 'em your card and they said they'd get up with you. I told 'em I was just a country doctor, and I left all the negotiations to you."

There was an audible sigh on the phone. "Thank goodness. You have a tendency to play all your cards too early."

"Yes, sir."

Chevalier and Ruby drove for a while before either spoke. "Can you believe that guy?" Ruby asked. "Do we have an interest in market share in Harvey County? What kinda question was that?"

"One he already knew the answer to, Royce." Chevalier laughed out loud. "This is gonna be more fun than swimming with the rich and famous and the dolphins. I assure you that doctor isn't as naïve as he pretends he is."

"I don't think he is, either," Ruby replied.

Chapter Twenty Nine

Thrombley called Bones the next morning. "Okay, you made an impact."

"How's that?"

"You asked them if they had any interest in market share in Harvey County."

"I guess they thought I was a rube."

"Quite the contrary. They know quite well you knew the answer. They only had two choices with you. They could tell the truth and win your respect or lie and prompt me to call Novell for more options."

Bones chuckled. "It's a trick I learned from two men I respect, Martin Taylor, and you. Ask a question that you know the man knows for a fact. If he lies then you know you have to proceed with extra caution."

"We enter negotiations at ten. Only one word of wisdom. Now you have to turn it over to me. Some of the lower levels may try to call you and get you to make statements to compromise the position. Don't go for it."

"Charlie, if I haven't learned anything else I now know I am only a doctor, not a biz guy, or a negotiator. I will not tie your hands."

"Any last thoughts?"

"Hm. Well, I promised I wouldn't interfere but there is one thing."

"Which is?"

"When Riley Harper sent that early offer, I couldn't see anything in there about my employees, so I called him to ask. I wanted a five-year employment window for my key people. Sure, I had rules for them, too, no felonies, no inappropriate relationships, treat the patients with respect and dignity, et cetera.; the usual stuff."

"What was his response?"

"He said he was a biz guy. Said he could save five twenty-three per hour if he replaced my veteran nurses Lynn and Myrd with some kids right out of school. I told him they, along with docs here, are the lifeblood of the practice. They knew all the patients and they cared about them. One time Myrd passed a kidney stone at lunch and came back to work because she knew old lady Ezzins wouldn't have her breast exam if she wasn't there and the woman was two years overdue. Those kinds of folks can't be replaced."

"What did Harper say?"

"SOB said he was a businessman, not a sap. I told him take his five twenty-three an hour out of my hide but don't get rid of my people. I don't care if you give me eight million dollars, I can't take care of my patients without my people. If you take over and let 'em go, it'll hurt your business. What these guys forget is this is about people, not money. You start to treat people like dollars, and then your dollars will dry up one day. That sorry rascal Harper said you keep treating people like a fool and your money's gonna run out." Bones buried his head in his hands. "I really don't like that guy."

Charlie smiled. "He never had a chance with you, and I'm glad he failed. You needed to explore your options. You could still wind up with the old system, but I've got a feeling they are gonna have to decide if they want to serve Riley Harper's dreams or yours. I don't think they can have both. I'll update you every few days. I feel good about it. Sandhills seems to sense an opportunity here and I believe they will make the best of it."

"You know, Charles, these guys made more effort to understand my soul over one Italian supper than the old system did for twenty-five years of sweat equity. I don't get it."

"It's like a husband who lets a good wife get away. Sometimes people don't appreciate what they have until it's gone."

"Charles, one more thing, though. You know the Stark rules better than what I do. I do not want to exceed the Fed rules by even a penny. For one, I like to sleep at night. Number two, I know for a fact if we did it'd get back to Riley Harper and he'd have me tossed in Atlanta Federal Prison and I'd be a prisoner-doctor; they have a doctor shortage you know, and they know my Board Scores."

"Don't worry. I have no interest in stripes, either."

"They would go nice with that Del McCoury-style gray horse's mane of yours, though."

"Yeah, but they'd shave it off on intake and it took me a long time to grow it. Don't want to give up the second best hair in bluegrass now that I've earned it."

"Got it, boss. Hey, you remember Bee Bridges BBQ, don't ya?"

"How could I forget?"

"Tell you what. You get me a fair deal and I'll shake hands on a life-time annuity of Bees every time you set foot in Harvey County."

"Done deal." Charlie said, with a smile Bones could almost feel over the phone.

As it turned out, it was the best play Bones ever made. Maybe he wasn't all that bad at this negotiation thing after all.

Chapter Thirty

When Billy made partner, Bones was like a proud Papa. He told Peg they just had to have a party, and then left all the details to her as he always did. He was tireless in his promotion of the boy, though, and walked around town to pass out fliers and cigars like Billy was some kind of war hero.

Peg was a detail person who never failed to organize, and this event was no exception. She knew Bones' first order of business would be entertainment. "We can go without food, Peg, but we gotta have music," Bones would say.

Peg called the Darin and Brooke Aldridge Band and they cleared their schedule right away. "Wouldn't miss it, Peg," Darin said. "Chris is gonna be gone that day, but we'll get Brownie Scott to guest with us on the banjo."

Peg knew better than to have a party without food. Just 'cause Bones would forget to eat didn't mean the guests would see it the same way. She called in little Maggie, the best county cuisine caterer in Harvey County. "Why, honey, I'd be honored. After the way Doc Bones took care of Mama when she had heart failure . . . and why, that little Billy's gonna be just like him."

Morning broke the day of the party, all Carolina blue skies and fifty-ish temperatures. A few dogwood petals floated on a slight breeze; it was all just plum Southern perfect. Bones thought back to when he'd opened the office. He'd bought an old building that was two blocks down from the liquor store and backed up to the "Knob," a tough section of town. By any modern standards it was humble at best. The location was one no marketing guru would have ever deemed strategic, but home is where the heart is, and they'd been there twenty-five years. One day they had some repairs done to get ready to open the office, and the neighbors came out to watch. Tyrone Demetrius picked up a paint brush and pitched in.

"Appreciate the help, Tyrone," Bones said. "I know what you're thinking."

"What's that, Doctor?"

"Uh-oh, here comes that white boy. There goes the neighborhood."

Tyrone smiled and flung some flecks of paint off his brush in Bones' direction. "I'm gonna whitewash you, cracker!"

The docs ended up making good neighbors. Over time property values went up, but the character of the neighborhood was not degraded. Bones often went to the local Friday fish fries. So when Billy made partner, Tyrone Demetrius was the first person to call, and sent a bouquet of wild flowers for the occasion. "Sign me up for the party, Doc. You play good for a Caucasian."

"Will do."

And on Billy's Partner Party Day, Tyrone was there at 8:00 AM to help set up the tents and haul in gallons of Kate's famous sweet tea. Later in the day, Mayor Philbert showed up, took the stage for a minute, and asked all the dignitaries to raise their hands. Other than the mayor no official was there.

Tyrone punched Bones in the ribs and whispered in his ear. "Hey, Doc, I guess you only invited the important people."

"Dang right, Tyrone."

There might have been little official presence, but both sides of the acquisition battle sent silent representatives. They were unprepared for the spectacle. The staff turned the parking lot into a tent city that was almost a small version of the Harvey County Fair.

Brownie Scott surveyed the scene, and said, "Doc, I appreciate y'all getting together for something besides a funeral."

There were long tables with plates of deviled eggs, fried chicken, pickled peaches, and pimento cheese sandwiches just like what they used to have on Memorial Day at Harvey First Methodist. The paper table covers flapped in the breeze. It favored a family reunion or the church grounds on Memorial Day.

They played on under the cover in spite of a brief afternoon thundershower, except they made sure to take a break during the lightning. Tyrone sat in and picked the blues with Bones on a slow version of "Sitting on Top of the World" that sizzled as hot as the country stir-fry on little Maggie's grill. The music and the aroma of ribs and Polish sausages wafted through the neighborhood. Some came to thank their doctors for being there, some came to hear the music, and for some it was because they sure could use the free meal. The Harvey County Sheriff's Office sent a couple cars, but they weren't needed. The officers sat at the picnic tables and ate; Maggie's chow was the best. WNCW 88.7 came all the way from western NC to do a live radio feed.

Ace bluegrass DJ Dennis Jones surveyed the situation. "This is history, Bones. It ain't every day a new young doctor signs up for a lifetime in Harvey County, or *any* rural part of the state, for that matter."

"It was 'cause we have good music, Dennis. He's already hooked on both 'Going Across the Mountain' and 'The Gospel Truth.' Nowadays, when we can't get it with the giant rabbit ears, we catch it on Internet Stream."

The next morning, one of the Harvey Memorial Hospital VPs called Bones. "Doc, I gotta admit that was some kinda party. Where did all those people come from?"

"Where did they come from? Good Lord, those folks were our patients. Where do you think they came from?" Bones hung up the phone and scratched his head. *Just like Indie used to say. How in the world can you be in health care and not understand where those folks come from? Good Lord, if it weren't for patients, why the heck would we need to have a party?"* Bones just couldn't understand.

Chapter Thirty One

Peg beeped Billy at 10:00 AM. "Dr. Spurgeon, a new drug rep is here. She's bringing lunch today. Can she bring a menu by your office?"

"Sure. She's gotta hurry, though. I'm booked solid."

"Okay." Peg brought the rep up to Billy's office. The young lady sat down in the seat across the desk from Billy's chair.

"See ya, Peg." Billy waved as Peg went out the door.

Billy took a look at the rep. "I'm sorry. I don't remember you." He was certain he would have. Blond-haired, blue-eyed, beyond cute. *Dang, where do they get these kids? They look like escapees from cheerleader camp.* "Are you new?"

"Yes, sir." She placed a card on Billy's desk. "Anna. I'm with BU."

"Bluegrass Unlimited?" Billy laughed.

The girl blinked and looked off to the side. "No, sir. BU: Barometrics Universal. We're new in the States, but we've been in Europe for a decade. Our specialty is blood pressure. We are innovators in the field, and we are the best. We also have a minor interest in dermatologicals." She reached into her bag and put a few samples on the desk. "I'll leave these with you. Our new blood pressure medication is due out next month." She unfolded a large glossy Madison Avenue layout and began to address the highlights.

"Very well. Uh, I'm kinda busy. Can you leave me some promo material?"

"Sure. I'll leave this and also an article from JAMA. Are you aware of the new research on renin-angiotension disequilbrium?"

"Sure." Billy laughed. He recalled the lunch meetings at Chang's with Bones who'd tell him of old Dr. Bakerman's lectures on the subject. Bakerman would get so excited he'd pound himself in the chest and say, "Students, the day will come when a blood pressure medicine will intervene at this very step in the reaction." One time he hit himself so hard he fell down, but he jumped right back up, continued to lecture, and never missed a beat.

Billy wished he could have been there in those early, laid-back days at Sandhills. Bones swore he learned most of his Pathology from Bakerman over hot dogs and ping-pong. "Little dude could play," Bones would say.

"Sir? Sir?" The young lady waved at Billy.

"Oh, huh, uh, yeah, yeah, angiotension, yeah, I'm with you."

"Well, I'll be back in a month with samples. By the way, I also go by the nickname of The Kentucky Derby Kid. The code word is 'Real Quiet.' I have consulted with a Mr. Riley Harper. I trust you are familiar with him?"

"Uh, yes."

She leaned over the desk and offered Billy a menu. "I can bring lunch today. What would you like?"

Billy took a glance at her and then looked at the menu. "Hm. Let's see. Can I have the chicken tenders?"

She eased over and squeezed the office door shut, then sat back down and leaned out further across Billy's desk. *This girl's dress is cut low.* Two fleshy pink bobbers peeked out like a pair of fishing lures on a line. She stretched out farther, arched her back a bit, and pulled her shoulders back. "Now, Dr. Spurgeon, or uh, may I say Billy? I want you to know if you write my blood pressure medicine you can have anything you want..."

The sweat popped out on his brow and Billy stopped for a moment. "Uh." He took one last look.

She smiled. "And now that I have your attention, Mr. Harper asked I bring this paperwork by for you to look at."

"What is it?"

She moved closer and rubbed up against him. "Billy. You must understand. These big medical systems aren't interested in old doctors like Bones Robertson. For that matter, neither am I." She began to massage his neck. "Mr. Harper is willing to advance you two hundred fifty thousand dollars if you sign this letter of intent with CMA."

"What does that mean?"

"If the other doctors sign with CMA you keep the money. If the other doctors are unable to see the wisdom of alignment with CMA, you still keep the money and we'd set up a new multi-specialty clinic and make you the first partner."

"But I just made partner here."

"Billy, Billy, you must leave behind these antiquated ways of doing business. You're the one they want and you're the one I want." She began to unbutton his shirt buttons and rubbed his chest wall. "Remember the code word, Billy. If you stay real quiet you can have anything you want and you can have it right now."

The sweat poured off his brow and his chest began to pound.

Peg beeped the office. "Billy, Angie is on line one. She asked if you were still gonna take her to lunch. She said she could be here in fifteen minutes."

"Yes. Tell her to come on. I'll be ready." Billy turned to the rep. "Look, lady, we have an open-door policy here and I'm gonna meet my wife for lunch. Uh, you're gonna have to leave and—"

She stood up, snuggled close, and mashed her breasts firmly into his side. "My offer stands. It's nice to see some young doctors for a change. Can we meet another time?"

"I don't think that'd be a good idea, but I'll look at the paperwork."

"Please do, and remember if you stay real quiet, I'm yours."

"I don't see how I could forget."

She pulled off Billy's tortoise shell glasses, put them on his desk, then kissed him several times and smeared lipstick all over his face. "I do hope this isn't our last visit." She straightened up her dress and scurried down the hall. She met Peg and handed her the menu. Peg walked on back to her office.

Bones drove up in the parking lot as the rep was leaving. He walked in to the office to hand Peg some mail.

"Dr. Robertson, what are you doing here on Wednesday? You not playing golf?" Peg asked.

"Rained too hard last night; they closed the course for the day. Decided to run some errands." Bones sorted through his mail. "Bills. Nothing but bills. One of these days we're gonna get banjo strings." He laughed. "Hey, who was that new girl?"

"The rep?"

"I guess. Had a big satchel. One of those fancy rolling ones. Young, cute thing, blond."

"I dunno. She talked to Billy."

Bones scratched his head. "The child looks familiar. I've seen her somewhere."

Peg looked up. "You know what? She was gonna bring lunch but Billy had already promised Angie, so she left. Oh, well."

Bones dropped by Billy's office. "Man, what happened to you?"

"Oh, nothing. Nothing, thank goodness. Hey, that was the Kentucky Derby Kid."

"That wasn't the Kentucky-Derby Kid."

"Are you sure? She knew the code word was Real Quiet."

"I'm positive. KDK is brunette; this kid was a blonde. I've seen her somewhere, just can't place her. What did she want?"

"A lot of things but I didn't give in. Swear I didn't. I told her I had to leave; Angie was coming for lunch. She had some paperwork she left behind from Riley Harper."

"Riley Harper? Son, we have been infiltrated."

Bones looked over the document. Suddenly Bones realized where he'd seen her. "Man, I know where I've seen that girl. She was the one who rode up here with Riley Harper the time they came to look at the practice." Bones looked at the paperwork. "Sorry rascal sent his chick as bait. Good Lord." He looked up at Billy. "You're a wreck. You better go clean up before Angie gets here. I'm glad you didn't go and make the mistake of a lifetime, boy."

"Uh, yeah, me, too."

Chapter Thirty Two

Billy sifted through the morning mail. One letter stood out. It was from William Wilder and Associates, was sent by certified mail, and did not have the appearance of a form letter. Billy remembered his lessons from Bones who always advised to be sure to scan the mail for lawyer letters. Most of them would be about Social Security disability claims or automobile accidents but every decade or so one would have a subpoena for a deposition regarding medical care. These were more apt to cause worry. Billy went to check with Bones and get his opinion.

Bones looked over the request. "Well, Billy, first of all I'm not too surprised Rick Lester would file. I suspect he would if he had a toenail fall off; he's always been an argumentative sort. There are several things about this case that I find in your favor. First of all, and most important, I really do not believe you have any true malpractice exposure here. Second, I'm not familiar with William Wilder and Associates. I sat on the malpractice review board for a number of years and his name never came up. That means he is either new to the business or never had any significant success in it, either of which is good for you. If you like, I'll run it by Martin Taylor. We get together every so often. If he thinks you have significant exposure I'll go ahead and ask him if he would sign on as a consultant. If he doesn't, then you probably do not have much to worry about. Taggert will likely be on your team right from the get-go. She looks like a little rag doll, but don't be fooled. That woman is tough enough to play poker with Snookers Molesby at the B and B. I wouldn't worry too much yet."

"Easy for you to say," Billy replied.

"I understand. There's no such thing as a trivial lawsuit. But remember what we say here at the office: "Don't worry 'til Bones says worry."

"I'll try." Billy smiled and stuffed the subpoena in the envelope and put it in his pocket. "I sure am glad we're on the same team."

"Me, too, Billy."

Bones already had plans to be at the coast at the end of the month, so he called Martin Taylor to see if he was going to be at his condo.

"Good to hear from you, Bones. Sure, come visit. Let's tee it up at Bogue Banks that Saturday."

"Great," Bones replied.

Chapter Thirty Three

After nine at Bogue Banks, the two went to their usual watering hole, Tony's Sanitary Fish Market.

The waitress took their orders. "Bones? I know you. It's fish but no bones, prefer steamed shrimp in butter, and a room overlooking the sound so you can watch the wild ponies run. And extra sweet tea and hushpuppies."

"Yes, ma'am."

"That's exactly what you had last time," Taylor observed.

The waitress spoke up. "It's like his daughter says: 'Daddy, some things never change and you're one of 'em.'"

Martin laughed out loud. "I've known this man since he got out of residency. You don't have to tell me. You're right, other than reading a ton of books and learning a bunch of new medicines, he's not one whit different." Martin smiled. "Still hits that low trap hook, though. If I could get him to learn a power fade I think he could knock two more strokes off his handicap."

"How did your golf game go today?" she asked.

Martin tugged on his tie lapel. "Slick again."

"Pardon?"

"Means all even," Bones said.

She left to get the plates. Bones laid out a folder with the documentation and went through Billy's case. Taylor read every word.

"So, whaddaya think?" Bones asked.

"Hm. His writing sure is better than yours."

"I concede, Counselor. His odds?"

"I agree with you. He made the right choices and the system didn't follow through and plus the patient didn't follow instructions. Your boy doesn't have the liability here. But, never forget; a man was injured, and juries never forget. I don't think it will get to court; it'll settle. It is possible after reading the tea leaves Billy will be best off to offer something nominal but it has a long ways to go before any decision such as that. Don't sign without talking to me first."

"Yes, sir."

"With Taggert as lead counsel of the insurance carrier on your team, and Wee Willie Wilder as the plaintiff's, I don't think you have much to fear. My boy Gibson said Taggert about dismembered Wilder last winter in a heart attack case we'd surely reached a settlement on, and the patient went home empty-handed. Wilder's a divorce attorney and doesn't really understand the malpractice business. Tell Billy there's always concern, but to have no fear."

"You know, Martin, Lester was always a jerk to Billy and everyone else, for that matter, but we all feel sorry about what happened to him. Billy would like to tell him so, but the team won't allow it."

"Let me send the message through channels," Taylor said. "Trust me, they are terrified of empathy."

"Okay, boss. Good to see you again."

"Always."

How's Gib?"

"Fine."

"Tell him I want him to carry on the tradition. We need all the honest lawyers we can get in this old world."

"I'll do it."

They shook hands and left for the evening.

Chapter Thirty Four

185

Wilder called Taggert on Tuesday. "Good morning."

"I suppose."

"Come on, Taggert. Look at it this way: If it weren't for litigation, we wouldn't have a job."

"To the physicians, and I'm sure the patients would agree, as one of my doctors always says, 'There is no such thing as a trivial lawsuit.'"

"God, they take it so personally. It's only a business. I'd like to call a settlement conference. Would your client consider reasonable solutions? Look, everyone knows Mr. Lester is going to prevail in this matter; we might as well get it over with."

"And end your billable hours? Heaven forbid. Not like you, Will. And yes, Lester may prevail, but not against my client. Dr. Spurgeon has no exposure and documented his actions quite well."

"How 'bout next Wednesday?" Wilder asked.

"I'll check and see."

Taggert called Billy. "I think we should meet. I don't believe he has much of a hand, but we need to see what cards he thinks he has."

Billy agreed. "I'm already tired of fooling with it. Like you've said, I don't have much exposure, and I sure don't want to get stuck with the entire tab. Even though Lester is a jerk, you can understand why the man is pissed. He had a headache but was neurologically intact when I ordered the CT, then we can't find him, and he's hemiplegic the next time I lay eyes on him. I feel like the ER will definitely have to settle. They should have ordered a stat CT before I ever even saw him. If they had, none of the rest of us would even be here today. I'm a little softer on the hospital, but if they'd called the report on Saturday as ordered we mighta caught him before he left town. I believe they'll have to settle, too. Some of the employees knew, or should have known, to go find that CT report."

Billy thought back to what Bones had told him at Chang's Chinese. "Bones said way back in the Bonfield case that the Croatan Community Hospital made promises and then reneged. Can we trust Harvey Memorial to follow through?"

"Bones and his stories. The man had a memory." Taggert smiled. "And we do, too. I agree. No one has forgotten those tactics, and no, I don't trust Jackson Leggett either. He has been lead counsel for both Croatan and Harvey Memorial Hospital for years, and he is quite predictable. Willie Wilder borders on incompetent. We just have to lay back and see what develops."

Billy recalled Bones' pregame scouting report on Taggert; feminine but still plenty tough. She'd even played cards with Snookers at the B and B. "Sort of like playing poker, huh, Taggert?"

She rolled her eyes. "You been talking to Bones?"

Billy smiled. "Yes, ma'am."

"Yep; a lot like poker. Let's go and see how it plays out. Just keep your cards close to the vest, understand?"

"Got it. I'm even better at that subter-fuging business than Bones."

"Lord help me," Taggert mumbled.

The settlement conference was set up for a Wednesday at the Holiday Inn. The lawyers grumbled about the accommodations. Billy turned to Taggert. "Maybe if we don't upgrade they'll bypass us for better gigs. I asked Bones to come. Is that okay?" Billy asked.

Taggert laughed. "Might as well. It's on a Wednesday, and he's off. No way he's gonna stay home and leave you on your own anyway."

When they arrived Bones took one look at the line-up and called Billy out into the hall.

"What's up?" Billy asked.

"Man, we caught a break. That mediator is George Rice. He's a guitar man. He ain't bad for a lawyer."

"I don't recall seeing him around. Is he bluegrass?"

"No, but he's traditional. Russian folk music. Saw him at Ziggy's one time. Keep 'em busy with some chit-chat. I'm going back to the house to get my mandolin. Where's your banjo?"

"At the office."

"I'll be back in a minute."

Rice informed all the participants of the order of business. By protocol, the plaintiffs were allowed to go first. Wild Willie Wilder was a rotund little man who looked like his pants would surely fall down if not held up by bright red suspenders. What hair he had was as jet black as if it'd been dyed with shoe polish and he had carefully arranged several strands of hair to try to cover his bald spot on the top. They looked as if they'd been painted on his scalp.

Billy turned to Taggert and whispered. "Not exactly gonna be up against Gregory Peck in the courtroom, ma'am."

She smiled. "Don't think it'll get that far, Doc."

Wilder's presentation was a bit overdone. Mr. Lester was an acceptable businessman, but the video that they'd put together to portray his life was like a movie production, complete with a violin orchestral soundtrack.

Bones returned near the end of the presentation.

Billy turned to Bones. "He wasn't in line for sainthood or anything. That violin was too formal and melancholy for my taste. I'da preferred Chubby Wise."

"Or Indie," Bones added.

Taggert saw it the same. "These are like movie trailers. They show you the important parts that might entice you to watch the whole show. They're gonna portray Lester as a fine businessman, who's been disabled by negligence. Did you notice they saved the venom for the ER? In fact, they hardly mentioned you at all, Billy."

"What do you make of it?"

"If they had anything on you, they'd already be touting it."

After a short break, the defendants were allowed the floor. The ER docs went first, and they allowed their legal team to speak for them. The tone was conciliatory.

Jackson Leggett was there for the hospital. As usual, he made the argument that doctors not hospitals make the mistakes and the institution should not be involved in the litigation. "Humans, not bricks and mortar, make errors. The hospital was unable to change the outcome."

Taggert passed a note to Billy. *They'll do what they can to settle.*

Taggert spoke for Billy and left no doubt he had no way to change the outcome.

Wilder presented for Lester and gave some kind of circuitous speech.

Rice then spoke again, and asked that everyone go to their prospective quarters to ponder the case, consider what they thought was right, and see if a consensus would develop that could bring the situation to resolution.

Bones passed a note to Billy. *He's saying: Please Search Your Heart.*

The various teams split up into different hotel rooms, Taggert opened the discussion in theirs. "Gentlemen, I don't have much doubt here that the ER is prepared to settle. In fact, if they don't, the message is clear: Wilder will pursue them aggressively."

"What the heck was Jackson's point?" Bones asked. "They never easily concede to the notion of 'systems failure." Policy and procedure can impact the ability to secure good outcomes. It can sound a bit theoretical to juries but is a hundred percent true. I don't think the hospital can dodge the failure to call an abnormal CT as ordered."

"The legal term for his argument is BS, gentlemen. I don't think Jackson is here in good faith. He didn't mention they forgot to call the CT report as ordered, did he? Don't worry; I'll continue to remind him until he can't forget. He's just gathering info and hopes for a way to wiggle out but I don't think he's gonna fool too many of 'em." Taggert was always the realist.

"It looks like Wilder didn't have much to say about me." Billy mused. "I wonder if they have some secret up their sleeve."

"Not likely," Taggert answered. "These previews are coded messages about where they are headed. Wilder doesn't think he has anything on you."

"Then why don't they just drop me now?" Billy complained.

"Well, if they did, you can be sure Jackson Leggett would blame you endlessly until this was all over. He would make the case all the way to final arguments that Wilder blamed the wrong party. Ironically, by staying in it for now, your reputation stands to take less of a beating by your home team hospital. God bless Jackson for protecting you." She forced a wry grin.

"It's called 'Empty Chair Syndrome,' Billy," Bones counseled.

Taggert shook her head. All these years, and still dealing with Bones. She slapped him on the back. "I gotta hand you one thing, Bones. You're solid loyal. You won't ever lay down. No quit in ya."

"Yep." Bones flashed a wide smile of teeth that were fairly white for his age.

"So, what do we do now?" Billy asked. "I sure would like to get this over with."

"Patience, my boy," Taggert replied. "We do what lawyers do all the time; wait." She pulled out a book to read.

Bones and Billy followed their usual strategy too; they always did when they were nervous, they played music. Bones motioned toward the bed. "I brought your banjo."

"Cool." Billy went to get it out of the case.

"In times of trouble, we don't drink whisky," Bones said, "we play music. Come to think of it, one old fiddler asked why we couldn't do both." He began to tune up. "I told him us docs better stick to music. If I was a drinker to any degree, I'm sure these lawyers would use it against me."

Bones got out his mandolin and they struck up "Sally Goodin."

A call came that Rice was on the way and Taggert made them put the instruments up. They rested the cases on the bed, and tried to put on their best game face.

Mr. Rice came in and sat down. For a while he probed around for a potential dollar figure the group thought might be appropriate. Bones and Billy had no idea and left it up to Taggert. Rice hinted as to how much exposure they thought Billy might have, and neither doc could answer with authority except to say they thought Billy was powerless to change the outcome and had ordered the right studies at the right time.

Rice glanced at the bed and spotted the instrument cases, which sparked a change of topic. "Do you play?" he asked.

"Sure," Bones piped up. "All of us except Taggert, that is. I think she can sing, though."

"Bones, this isn't one of your bluegrass shows," Taggert said.

"Can you play 'Rawhide'?" Rice asked.

"Sure." Bones got out his mandolin. "Billy here's getting good on the banjo. He's taking lessons from Brownie Scott."

"The IBMA champion?"

"Yep," Billy replied.

"I play guitar; I wish I had brought it." Rice's tone turned sociable.

"You're kidding," Bones said. "Hey, come to think of it, didn't I see you at Ziggy's one night? Russian folk music. Great fiddler with you."

"That was us, sure enough."

"I wish you'd brought your ax," Billy said.

Taggert later had to admit she didn't know what the term meant and had never heard any doctor tell a lawyer he wished they'd brought an ax to a settlement conference. Bones and Billy explained that "ax" was a bluegrass term for a personal musical instrument; in Mr. Rice's case, a guitar.

Somewhere in the session Rice let it slip that Wilder's experts had failed to implicate Billy.

Taggert took notes.

"Oh, Lord," Rice said. "That was a good 'un, Doc. Play one more." Rice was having a large time (bluegrass for a grand time). They struck up "Rag Time Annie" in honor of Taggert, who favored a grown-up red-haired rag doll, and then they played "Jenny Lynn."

Bones thought he heard someone at the door and held out his leg to indicate the final verse of the tune.

Rice went to the door. No one was there. "Hm. I guess I better get back over to Wilder's," Rice said. "I don't want to be accused of collusion. Did enjoy the session, though."

"Yeah," Taggert said. "I've come to know these bluegrass people. They are hard to whip. I guess it's 'cause they read so much."

Bones laughed out loud.

"Look, guys, I have to take a message back to Wilder," Rice said. "It's my job, you know. I know everybody lies to the mediator, but tell me some of what you think about this thing."

Bones jumped to his feet. "Look here, now, Mr. Rice. You're a guitar man, and I'm a mandolin man, and Billy there plays the banjo. We're bluegrass, and we don't lie to nobody, mediator or anybody else, for that matter. I've known Billy all his life. He don't tell no lies, and you and I both know he couldn'ta done a thing about this case. So our message to Wilder is *res ipsa loquitur*, by God!!"

Taggert all but rolled off the couch and doubled up in laughter. Bones paced around the room.

"*Res ipsa loquitur*. I've never had a doctor say that to me. They have coached you well," Rice responded.

"They didn't teach me that, and they ain't coaching Billy, either!"

Taggert seized the opening. "Let me interpret in legal terms, George." She glanced over at Bones. "Frankly, we believe Dr. Spurgeon has absolutely zero exposure in this case. At the same time, he wants to be sure Mr. Lester is treated fairly. I think we all know if he had been properly diagnosed in the ER, the outcome may have been significantly better. Here's our deal, George, and we won't back off it: We are confident the ER docs will have to settle. Retail on this injury is somewhere around a mil. They have that much coverage. If they settle for that much, although I'm certain they won't, end of game. If not, the hospital needs to ante up the balance. The only way Dr. Spurgeon might get involved would be if the ER and the hospital together can't get to something reasonable, say roughly two-thirds of retail. The rate increase breakpoint for Billy is a quarter mil, and we won't exceed that under any circumstances. We've worked together on a lot of cases, and you know I'm good for my word. As far as Jackson, given his past history, until he is signed, sealed, and delivered, I'm not yours, you follow?"

"Got it. I don't trust Leggett, and I don't think Will does, either. I know Martin Taylor never did. We'll see how it plays out." Rice was certain Wilder was going to drop Spurgeon once he had a deal on paper, but also knew that was more information than he could ethically give to Taggert. "I hate for an innocent man, especially a bluegrass man, to have to be dragged along in this thing, but for now there is no alternative. I hope you understand."

Billy smiled. "I don't believe in shooting the messenger, sir. Besides, I want to hear you pick that guitar."

Rice shook hands and left. Bones and Billy played a few more tunes while waiting on his next visit. "It's like Indie said," Bones noted. "He understood why Nero fiddled while Rome burned. There just wasn't anything else he could do for the time being."

Chapter Thirty Five

Peg beeped Bones. "Mr. Stanley is on line one."

"The hospital CEO?"

"Yes."

"Okay, I'll get it."

"Dr. Robertson, we are working behind the scenes with Mr. Thombley to try one last time to get these negotiations squared away so you can remain affiliated with Harvey Memorial."

"Yes, Mr. Thombley has kept me informed. I just don't understand business; I've left it all up to him."

"He's a very smart man."

"I agree."

"Between you and me, the arrangement that Raleigh has our lease, and that CMA is in charge of managing all of our practices' management . . . our family of doctors. I mean . . . well, this has put us in an awkward spot at times."

"I understand that, too."

"Can you come by the office at lunch? There is one concept I want to explore with you and no one else can answer it for you."

"Okay. I'm glad to listen but I have to tell you I don't make any business promises of any kind unless I run it by Mr. Thombley."

"Fine. After we discuss it, you can go over it with him."

"Fair enough."

They met at Stanley's door. "So, how are your negotiations coming along?" Stanley asked.

"Well, slow, but these things always are. So what's on your mind?"

"Come on in," Stanley said. Bones sat down. Stanley went to his desk. "We realize we will be making an error if CMA lets your practice get away. I wish to discuss a few more matters. These things are complicated now but we all have to be sure we are compliant with Stark Law. Compensation that is in any way tied to referrals is strictly forbidden and can have severe legal consequences."

"Yes sir. One reason I hired Mr. Thombley was to be sure I didn't inadvertently make that kind of error in the contractual language." Bones checked his watch. "I gotta get back to the office in an hour."

"Certainly." Stanley paged his secretary. "Hold my calls for fifteen."

"Yes, sir."

Stanley got up, closed the door, and went back to his desk. "Bones, you have to understand. Chick means well, but he can over-extend his authority at times."

Bones laughed. "So, he pissed off Riley Harper, huh?"

Stanley coughed. "No, no. It's just that in an organization like this we have to be accountable."

"I understand. My brother-in-law said the hardest part of being in the army was that sometimes you had to take orders from a fool just because he outranks you."

Stanley squirmed in his chair.

It was all Bones could do not to giggle.

Stanley reached in his brief case and pulled out some paperwork. "How's Billy's lawsuit going?"

"He's working on a building."

"Pardon?"

"In other words it is a work-in-progress, but he's getting there." Bones paused. "Never mind." Bones looked away a moment, then turned back to Stanley. "He's getting there. I think he'll be okay."

"These lawyers sure make it hard to stay in business. They insisted they had to add us on to the case. We didn't have any more to do with it than Billy."

"I understand."

Stanley sat back down. "Bones, are you aware our insurance has no deductible?"

"Explain."

"In other words, any payout we make is ours until we tap the co-insurance, right from the first dollar. We are the bottom line; the pocket."

"I see. And?"

"It is the exact opposite for you doctors. Your insurance covers the first dollar, and in fact everyone is careful to never exceed a doctor's insurance limits."

"Yeah, if they did, folks might start to find out what all's going on."

Stanley frowned. "I suppose." He paused. "Anyway, I think I can see a way clear for all of us here."

"How do you mean?"

"Well, you are the sole owner of the real estate for Harvey Family Practice, correct?"

"Yes."

Stanley flipped through some papers and turned to the contract. "Do you realize you have not charged enough rent through the years?"

"I liked having partners more than having money. You know what they call doctors who don't treat their partners well?"

"What's that?"

"Solo practitioners."

Stanley fell silent for a moment, then went on. "Well, Bones, there's no reason you can't have it both ways. We've studied this entire predicament in detail. Chick even talked to Senator Walton. We feel like the deal should acknowledge this underpayment and make restitution for this debt you are owed."

"Yeah, I appreciate you looking out for me. Just how do you propose we do that?"

"We believe we can leave the current deal on the table level as Chick outlined it, except now we give you a full half million for your real estate."

Bones took off his glasses, polished them with a cloth, and narrowed his gaze. "How, pray tell, are you going to do that? At least three independent appraisals put the building at three hundred grand at best." He laughed. "In all my experience with negotiations, which is limited, I've never had anyone offer me more than something's value."

Stanley stood up, walked over to the window and looked out. "Very simple, Doctor. Very simple. We know you carry some weight with Physician's Liability Malpractice Insurance. We believe this Lester case will be resolved for a total of six hundred thousand and we are sure the ER doctors will be out two. I'm not sure how much harm that damn car dealer Lester was done, but he's a public figure and no one wants to go to court."

"I don't get what you're driving at."

"Bones, I know you are a man of your word. All of this is confidential, right? Just between me and you?"

"Sure, Mr. Stanley. I swear with my hand on a stack of HIPAA forms."

"We know you have PL's ear. Have, ever since the Bonfield case. All you have to do is convince PL that Billy can't hold up to the pressure in court, and that he'd be best off to settle at four hundred. He'd stay under the half mil that would get him in any real trouble. If Billy would testify the hospital is not the problem here, we're certain Wilder would drop us. Then we'd pay you an extra two for your building. Everybody wins. Billy's rate might go up a little, but we'll eat that when we take over the practice."

Yeah, Bones thought, *and charge it back to all the docs.*

Stanley continued. "He's not out of pocket so much as a dime and you'd get the fair market value of three hundred thousand for your real estate plus the extra two from this end of the deal which would remain confidential. We all win."

"And my partners?"

"They'll get the counteroffer Chick came back with; around four sixty for the docs to split and also we'd restore the ongoing contractual arrangements to the specs he first outlined. At near a half mil for the practice, it'd be the most lucrative deal we've ever done for a small group, and you'd have an extra two hundred to boot for your real estate. We should have signed it then and been done with it. That's the best offer the group is ever gonna get. You're the one we want, and you'll get the premium you deserve. It's only fair."

Bones walked over to the window and put an arm around Stanley's shoulder. "Let me be sure I've got it: Billy's insurance would pay Lester, Harvey Memorial would dodge any part of the lawsuit settlement, or at worst, might have some nominal number in the pocket to cover it if needed, and then you'd pass on half the savings to me. Is that right?" Bones knew the hospital must be concerned. They blew the case both in the ER and by failing to call the CT report on Saturday. He took it as a sign the hospital knew they would have to settle if an adequate deal were not struck with the other parties. "So Marvin, did I understand?"

"Exactly. What do you think?"

"Good God, Marvin. The answer is no. The practice is for sale, but Billy ain't. The answer is not just no, but *hell no!*"

Bones walked to the door and slammed it on the way out.

Why did the doctor gig ever have to turn into business, anyway? he thought.

Peg, the office manager, called out as Bones walked back in the office. "You okay, Doc?"

"Yeah, I'm okay." Bones sighed. "Just another day in the salt mines." He found his stethoscope, put some music on the office CD player, and went back to work.

Chapter Thirty Six

Bones called Taggert to let her know. "I promised confidentiality, but it was only on a stack of HIPAA forms," he said. He spilled out the details of the visit with Stanley.

Taggert took it in. "Damn," she said. "That is Jackson Leggett's signature work. I'll call Wilder. We are out or we fight to the death and he knows he doesn't have the cards."

"Just don't tell him how you came about the information," Bones said.

"Won't have to; he'll know."

Taggert called Wilder. "Will? We need to call an emergency meeting. Just me and you and Dr. Spurgeon."

"What's up?"

Taggert explained the circumstances.

"My goodness," Will replied. "So where do we go from here?"

"You might as well bring his release papers ready to sign."

"Okay."

Taggert and Billy met at lunch the next day. "What's up?" Billy asked.

"Today is gonna be a good day, just you wait and see, Billy."

Wilder arrived and plopped his briefcase on the table. He shook Billy's hand. "Due to new information we have secured, I have prepared the appropriate paperwork to secure your release from this case, Doctor."

"Really?"

"Yes. Our experts failed to implicate you."

"Okay. I never thought I did anything wrong."

Wilder began to get out his paperwork.

Taggert spoke up. "By the way, Will. Tell the other parties that our informant would not tell us all because he swore on a stack of HIPAA forms, but they would be well advised to settle out of court. If it were to get that far and the informant had his hand on a Bible that would trump the HIPAA forms every time and he would not hesitate to tell all. You should get a reasonable settlement."

"Will do." Wilder had Taggert look over the papers. She signed, Billy followed, and that was it; Billy was free.

Chapter Thirty Seven

Bones and Billy went to the office on a Saturday afternoon.

"Man, Billy, this deal has chewed up way too much time," Bones said. "I gotta catch up on my dictation. Let's catch up a little and take Kate and Angie out to eat about 7:00. "

"Sounds great." They walked into Billy Spurgeon's office first. "Look at all this paper." Billy sifted through a pile on his desk as high as his neck.

They both jumped when the secret line rang.

Bones looked at the phone. "Look there, Billy. Wonder who has that number? It hasn't rung in a decade."Bones picked it up.

A near breathless, husky but feminine voice with a Mediterranean flavor answered. "This is the Kentucky Derby Kid. This is the first Saturday in May, 1998." 'My Old Kentucky Home' blared away in the background. "Today is the one hundred twenty-fourth running of The Kentucky Derby. I trust you gentlemen have a television set in your place of business?"

"Sure," Bones replied.

"I know you do. Your Del McCoury says it is in the break room. Go turn it on now."

"Hey, wait a minute. How do I know you're the real Kentucky Derby Kid?" Bones asked.

"Ask me a question."

"Do you ever ride in a car alone with Del McCoury?" Bones asked.

"I love his music, but I have never met him, or worked a gig with him, so no, I never have."

"No, I don't mean the real Del, I mean the one who looks like him."

"Know him well, have seen pictures. Love the hair. Never met him in person, either, but we work together on a regular basis via the messenger model. And no, I've never ridden out with him to work a case."

"Why?" Bones asked.

"The messenger model works without risk to the participants. And there are other reasons."

"Such as?"

"Long legs," she purred. "Dark brunette hair, cinnamon olive skin, part Latino, part Spanish, background in European espionage. Need confidentiality to maintain effectiveness. But more than anything, I suppose it's the legs. Your man has no clause in his contract to allow for such as me to be in his car alone with him."

"Yeah, I remember he said he was a good negotiator, but not that good."

"Correct."

"Don't blame him. My Kate wouldn't sign that either and I don't blame her."

"Kate is a smart woman."

"Sure enough."

KDK went on. "Well, you boys better catch the race. I have four hundred fifty-seven grand on Real Quiet. If RQ turns up a winner, then sign as soon as your Del man confirms."

"Will do," Bones said, and hung up the phone.

They turned on the set. The announcer came on and Bones turned up the TV.

The announcer cranked it up. "They're at the post. Real Quiet gets off to an awkward start."

Bones groaned.

"And Favorite Trick is coming up on the outside...and man, oh man, that horse just got knocked back by...let's see...that was Indian Charlie."

Bones jumped up and cheered. The announcer resumed. "Boy, did that knock Favorite Trick out of the battle for a minute there," he crackled across the air. Bones laughed out loud. "'Indian Charlie!' That had to be a shove from old Indie!" Bones yelled out loud.

"Rock'n'Roll's charging on the outside," he broadcast.

"Hey, you played some of that music as a kid, Bones, not too bad."

"Yeah, at least as long as it's classic, and he doesn't win, he's okay with me for a place or show."

". . . And National Loar is falling behind . . . ."

"Glad we ain't trying the Mandolin Case." Billy and Bones shook with laughter.

". . . Rock'n'Roll's now dropping back . . . ."

"Not too far," Bones shouted, "just don't win. Go Real Quiet! GO!" Bones bit his nails.

"And they're on the back stretch and . . . and with three furlongs left its Real Quiet coming up on the outside . . . ."

"Go hoss, go!" Billy shouted.

"And the top of the stretch it's Real Quiet by a nose. Favorite Trick is gaining ground on the rail and . . . OH MY GOODNESS, did that horse take a shove in the flank by the filly Girl Scruggs. Who says the ladies can't be both feminine and tough? Why the classy lady has Favorite Trick strung to that rail tighter than a fifth string on a railroad spike capoed to C! Favorite Trick looks spent, y'all. Lawd have mercy, Girl Scruggs has got the fire in her belly; she ain't gonna let Favorite Trick get by. Yes, sir, buddy!"

Bones and Billy jumped up and cheered.

"And they're at the eighth pole and it's Real Quiet by two lengths. He's looking a bit leg weary, though. Can he make it? He's near the line. Yes! He's slowing, though, no question. Has he got enough? Has he got enough? Yes, it's Real Quiet at the wire. He's at the line and . . . YES! It's Real Quiet! Real Quiet is the winner of the one hundred twenty-fourth Kentucky Derby!"

Bones and Billy bear-hugged and danced a jig. "All we gotta do is wait on Charles," Billy said.

"Yep, it ain't over 'til Del sings."

The secret line rang again.

A high tenor singer's voice pierced the air. Bones held up the phone and Billy scrunched in to listen. "A snake tried to get in your house. You got him out——"

"Hey!" Bones shouted. "Was that our Del or Del McCoury?"

"'Tis me," Thombley replied.

"Man, you've not only got hair like him, you're starting to sound like him."

"Thanks. Okay, done deal with Sandhills. Here's the outline: Four seventy-eight up front for the docs to split. I have been through the on-going employment contracts line-by-line. Truth is, I red-lined very little; it was solid from the onset. There were just a few items that didn't apply because of your geographic location, but the boilerplate was far better than Chick's deal, at least after it got undermined. The real estate provisions are acceptable, too; fair market value both in rent and sale of your property should they build a bigger facility. I'll be glad to drop by next week for a formal meeting and you can call if you have any questions, but this agreement is fine. I'd rate it at ninety-eight percent of Stark, and you want to leave a little on the table so they feel good about the relationship going forward."

"I'm sure if we exceeded it, Riley Harper'd find out somehow and turn us in anyway."

"Well, you are clear with this deal. Look for confirmation via UPS two biz days; should be in by Tuesday. Here is your tracking number. Have all four partners sign and have Peg notarize. Return to Sandhills via secure courier. Fed Ex or

UPS is fine. Do wait until legal signs off, though; that'll be no more than seven business days. Congratulations, you have crossed the finish line in Acquisition Syndrome. Yours is a small practice. I have worked bigger cases, but never had as much fun in one."

"Thanks Del, or uh, Charlie. You're the best. I now owe you a lifetime annuity at Bee Bridges BBQ."

"Mercy, better than money in the bank," Charles replied.

"See ya soon, pal."

"Will do."

Chapter Thirty Eight

Ginger cracked open the door to her boss's office. "Riley? Mr. Williford is on line one."

"What does he want?"

"You. Otherwise, I don't know."

"Okay, okay." Harper picked up the phone.

"Riley? I need you up here now. It is urgent."

"Yes, sir." Harper got up from his desk and started toward the elevators. "I'll probably be back in ten minutes. No one gets much of that man's time. Hold my calls."

"Yes, sir."

Harper went up to Williford's office and the secretary offered him a seat across from the CEO's desk. In a moment, Williford was there. Harper started to get up.

"Keep your seat, Riley. What is this I hear about Harvey Family? Surely they are not going to defect."

"Uh, well, I am sure they did enter negotiations with Sandhills."

"See to it we secure that practice. What is the problem here?"

"Bones Robertson."

"How?"

"He is not responsive to our usual offers. We would have this signed by now if not for his stubbornness."

"Well, intervene, and I mean now." Williford reached over and picked up a thick stack of papers and tossed them in Harper's lap. "This study just came in from Sun Health out of Atlanta. I commissioned it. Projections are we will lose multiple millions of dollars in referrals over the next decade if we let this practice get away."

"Sir, I tried. This one is ill-fated."

"Well, try harder. Go to Robertson and offer him a million dollars outside the regular deal. We won't tell his partners."

"Sir, we don't need to establish such a precedent. If Bones Robertson tells anyone, we could see a lot of trouble from the Feds."

"He won't; too uptight about rules. He'd worry he might get in trouble."

"We need to worry that he might. A million is hard to hide."

"Oh, I can run it through our charitable arm. In an organization this size, it is easy to launder that much."

"I don't know, Mr. Williford."

"I do. Make it happen."

Harper shook hands and left.

Chapter Thirty Nine

"Dr. Robertson? Chick Crawley on line one."

"Thanks, Peg. I'll get it."

"Bones?"

"Yep?"

Chick hesitated. "Man, I know the taillights have about gone over the hill, but we need to talk this over one last time."

"Riley Harper on your butt?"

Chick sighed. "Man, just trying to do my job."

"I understand, Chick. You're a survivor."

"I dunno. I may get canned after this one."

"Where you want to meet?"

"May as well get a golf game out of it; might be our last one."

Bones chuckled. "Ah, Chick, don't worry. After this I'll be able to get us on at Sandhills CC."

"Yeah, that's what worries me. Good Lord, Bones. How 'bout Harvey County Club one time, for old time's sake?"

"Okay, but I always love River Run."

"Ah, come on, Bones. You gotta at least make it look like I tried to influence you."

"Okay, pal. The Club it is. I've been meaning to play it since they re-did number seven, anyway. I heard the new green has some changes in the breaks. I need to know all I can in Harvey County."

"God, no one knows the landscape better. Why CMA couldn't see it, I'll never understand."

Bones smiled. "It's easier to see from the street than it is from tall buildings. There's a reason Hartford didn't want to create his repertoire from sky-scraper cafeterias."

"John Hartford as in "Gentle on My Mind?"

"That's the one. I knew him a little. He knew true music was seldom created from the minds of executives who had high-rise offices; it was about regular people. Primary care medicine is as much art as science and much the same way; it's about people. A guy like Riley Harper will never get it."

"I understand, but idealism won't pay all the bills."

"Exactly why I needed you guys, or someone like you. I can only speak to the dynamics of primary care; that is all I am an expert in. I wouldn't know where to start to get a fair price on a new MRI machine."

"I'm gonna call Riley Harper's boss."

"Randolf Williford? Chick, that could be a risk if Harper gets in trouble. I still think he'll come back and try to put the blame on you for this whole fiasco."

"I don't care. I'm not gonna not pull out every stop and let you get away."

"I feel sure we'll sign with Sandhills; they have been straight up the whole way, but okay, go ahead. See, what CMA missed is this simple fact: They are big money players in the new health care biz world, the kings and queens. I know I'm just a peon and a pawn, but they forgot one thing: If you ain't got pawns you can't play chess."

"Let me meet with you after I touch base with Williford. Wednesday, ten o'clock, okay?"

"Sure. I always enjoy a visit at the Chick Coop."

They visited at Chick's office, went to the Club, played a quick nine, and left for lunch at the Billiard and Bowl. When they arrived, Minnie the Myna called out with her signature ambulance siren for Bones and a rooster crow for Chick. The meeting was somber. In spite if it all, Chick had been honest and was a true friend; a man Bones knew he could talk turkey with. Bones knew the acquisition was CMA-directed, and not Chick's fault.

Chick picked at his French fries and finally spoke. "Bones, I hate to see it turn into an all-out war."

"It won't for us, Chick. You are still on my loyalty list and I have a bunch of friends at Harvey Memorial. Harper didn't leave me any choice; I had to go with Sandhills, but that doesn't mean you guys and Raleigh won't get any of my business. For me, choice is patient-driven. I always send the patients where they want to go if their insurance will allow it."

"Well, I'm sure it will start out that way. But over time there will be an erosion of referral patterns. Sandhills will build a big multi-specialty clinic and put cardiologists and other specialists in there. Patients will try them out and some will change. Say you haven't signed yet?"

"No, it's not over 'til Del sings."

"Huh?"

"Waiting on legal for final confirmation; should be in seven to ten biz days by certified mail." Bones hesitated. "I just remembered I'm not supposed to tell yet, but that's the skinny. I know they sent you on reconnaissance, so toss 'em a little bone; maybe they'll stay off your tail."

Chick ordered a couple beers. He handed one to Bones. "Look pal, here's the message. Harper's gonna contact you."

"Riley Harper's gonna call me? You're kidding." Bones feigned surprise.

"I don't think he wanted to. Williford made him do it."

Bones reached over for one of Chick's fries.

"Man, we're old friends. I'm worried for you. Harper says he'll bury you," Chick said.

"Sort of like Khrushchev banging his shoe on the U.N. table, I reckon."

"Really, Bones, those guys are powerful."

Bones took a sip of his beer. "Let me ask you something, Chick. You don't think this is like dealing with the mob, do you?"

"No, it's not that bad. Nah, they won't kill you, but yeah, they are bad actors."

"If they were mob guys, I guess I'd just pack up my family, move on, and get an alias. But short of that level of devious, I'll just have to take my chances. All my friends are here, and I have no desire to leave. I need to take care of my patients, and they need me, too."

"I tried to tell 'em it won't work, but . . . ."

"What wouldn't work?"

"Harper said to tell you that if you wouldn't go along with him, he'd come down here to compete with you and take all your patients away."

Bones laughed out loud. "Harper's gonna compete with a country doctor? Good Lord, Chick. I break bread with my people and play music with them. Play golf with 'em, too. How can a man who works in tall buildings and wears a suit and tie compete with a country doctor as far as patients? He . . . . Uh. Heck, he doesn't know a thing about being a doctor. Until you've spent a life-time of rectal exams by day and prayers by night that you haven't overlooked an occult prostate cancer, there's no way to understand."

"He doesn't care about patients. All he cares about is money."

"I am sad to agree; you are correct." Bones said. Bones went to the B and B door that opened to the front room and called for Lou. Minnie called out the ambulance siren. Bones looked over at her. "No fear, Minnie. Everything is okay. Hey, Lou, how 'bout a couple cups of B and B coffee?"

"Sure thing, Doc."

Lou brought two cups to the table. "One straight for Doc, bluegrass coffee. One 'Candy coffee' for Chick, cream and two sugars—"

Bones clasped Lou's arm. "It's okay, Lou. He's one of us. The big boys tried to get him in a vice lock, but don't worry. I've got it covered." Bones reached in his pocket and produced a small, wrapped gift, walked back over to Chick, and handed it to him.

"What's this for?" Chick buried his head in his hands. "Man, am I gonna catch hell. I lost the acquisition."

"No, you didn't, Chick. CMA did it for you. It wasn't your fault."

Chick unwrapped the present like a small boy at a family birthday party. He broke into a huge peal of laughter. "A can of WD40! Doc's gonna get me right out of that vice lock when the time comes. Man, am I gonna need this."

Bones smiled. "Yes sir, brother. When they try to put you in the old Bolo Eagle Claw-hold, I know the boys who'll come to your defense."

"Thanks, Doc. Might need 'em before my career is over."

Bones hollered out to Lou. "Lou, one more cup for Chick."

"More candy coffee?"

"No, make it bluegrass."

"Yes, sir."

Chick turned to Bones. "Hey, you gotta admit I did learn some of your ways."

"Yep, Chick. We'll always be friends, don't worry."

"That's good." Chick smiled. He looked at Bones again. "Honest to goodness, man, I worry about you going up against them. Riley says he's gonna set up one deal after another and squeeze you out over time."

Bones laughed. "Tell you what, Chick. How 'bout you send him a return message?"

"What's that?"

"You tell Harper I know he's more powerful than me, and he's got a whole lot more money than I'll ever understand, let alone see. I know he drives a Porsche and he knows I drive a truck. But Grant had a lot more money and power than Lee, but look at what it took to kick Lee's ass. I'm sure he can do it over time, but why would he want to? Tell him I said that's stupid."

Chick sighed and patted Bones on the shoulder, then chuckled. "How did a little country boy get so dang contrary?"

Bones laughed. "It's the bluegrass way. Riley Harper lowering himself to talk to me. Imagine that. Williford must really be on his butt."

Chapter Forty

The next day, Riley Harper called Bones on his cell. "Dr. Robertson?"

"Yes?"

"This is Riley Harper."

Bones held the phone away from his ear for a moment, looked at it from arm's length, and then finally put it to his ear, and answered. "You're kidding."

"No, it's me."

"Well, Mr. Harper, I think the gig has played out. What in the world do you want from me now?"

"Ah, Dr. Robertson, you are a worthy adversary."

"I didn't know we were supposed to be adversaries, but okay, if you say so."

"But Doctor, surely you understand. These things are like war. And we warriors understand why things have to be as they are. Warriors understand each other, correct?"

"If you say so, Mr. Harper. What's your point?"

"I think we ought to meet to settle our differences."

"Meet?"

"Yes, how about tomorrow?"

"Mr. Harper, I've wasted too much time on this and been away from home way too much already."

"But we must, we must. I have reserved seating for two at the Capitol Club. It's the finest in Raleigh; we have a five-star chef, and it is also the best view of the city. It's on me."

"Hm. My Kate is gonna be at a baby shower tomorrow at lunch, otherwise I'd have to decline. Okay, I'll give you one hour at lunch, but it'll have to be here in Harvey County. I just don't have enough time to get all the way to Raleigh. So, Harvey County or nothing. No tickee, no washee."

Harper groaned. "If you insist. Where shall we meet?"

"Harvey Billiard and Bowl. Twelve-thirty. Ask for Lou. He'll get us a private table in the back."

"Gad."

"Sir?"

"Uh, I'll be there." Harper confirmed.

Bones thought about the call as he hung up. He remembered reading about Colonel James Stockdale's confinement in a POW camp. The worst guard of all, the one who had tortured him unmercifully met with him one day and went on and on about why he had done all the things he did to Stockdale. He called him "Stawdale." He said something like "Stawdale, you see we understand each other because we are both warriors. In war, warriors do what they have to do. They all understand this. After war is over, then bygones be bygones."

Stockdale knew what it meant. Sure enough, in two days they were liberated by the GIs. He never saw the prison guard again.

Riley Harper arrived in his black Porsche at 12:30 sharp. Ginger was on his arm as he walked through the gravel parking lot. She stumbled in her heels.

Lou met them on the front steps. "You'll have to check the chick at the door, Mr. Harper."

"She's my secretary."

"I don't give a damn if she's Cleopatra, and besides, I know who she is. Look here, child, if you was my young'un I'd tell ya to kivver up. And if you keep parading them jugs around one day some man with bad intentions is gonna get hold of you."

"Well, I never."

"Yes, you have. And let me tell you one more thing. You ever get after our Billy again, like I heard about, I'm gonna kick your skinny a--. . . . Well, Mr. Harper, if she comes in the B and B there is no meeting, got it?"

Harper sighed. "Okay." He snapped his fingers at the child like she were some kind of dog. "Go to the car. Stay."

"But, baby—"

"Hell, no. Go, I said, then stay."

Ginger began to cry but obeyed and wobbled across the gravel to the Porsche. Lou felt sorry for her all of a sudden and went to assist her to the car. He opened the door for her.

"Thank you, sir." She smiled. "You're kinda cute."

"Drop it, kid. I'm married to the one they call the second-best looking woman in bluegrass, and she's number one in our crib. You cause me any trouble, and Lord have mercy you talk about a woman's wrath!"

Ginger climbed in the passenger seat without another word.

Lou called Harper to follow. Minnie the Myna began to sing Darth Vader's "Imperial March" as Lou led Riley to a seat.

"What kind of bird is that?" Harper asked.

"Oh, that's just Minnie. She's a 'watch bird' of sorts. Just lets us know who has come by to visit. Bones'll be here in a minute. You have forty-five minutes. That's it. By the way, we got us a driving range now. Snookers Molesby is out back hitting shags right now."

"Who's that?"

"You don't want to know," Lou replied.

Bones cracked open the door and walked in. Minnie let out her ambulance siren imitation. "Hey Doc, Bull Wilson is out there shagging some balls for Snook," Lou said.

"Cool! Strong like bull. Tell him I'd love to see him before I split for the office," Bones said.

Lou took them to the private room in the back.

Bones turned to Harper. "Okay, Riley, let her rip. What you got to say that's so important?" Bones sat down across the table.

"Okay," Harper said. He turned to Lou. "May we have a minute of privacy? Business, you know."

Lou looked to Bones.

"Yeah, it's okay. Would you also tell Snook I want to hit some balls? I'll be out after a while."

"Dr. Robertson, I underestimated you, but I must inform you the higher-ups in the organization have authorized me to correct our failures in these negotiations."

"Lordy, Riley, don't you think it's a little late for that? You remind me of a girl who called the groom the night before the wedding, and said, 'Baby, why are you marrying her? I thought it was gonna be us.' The groom replied, 'Well, for one thing I love her, but the other is, I thought you made it pretty clear you weren't interested.' Generally folks tend to marry people who love 'em back."

Harper had been married six times and did not comment. "We are prepared to make an offer no one can touch. We are the most powerful health care entity in the Southeast, you know."

"So I hear." Bones nodded. "And my staff? What's in it for them? I never could get you to even listen to my dreams for them."

"Beg your pardon?"

"In the early days of negotiation you said on the phone you'd let my senior people go to save a few bucks. They've been with me twenty-five years; I can't abandon them. They have jobs and families and they have been loyal to the practice and the patients the whole way. Their loyalty has to be acknowledged in any arrangements I make."

"Oh, I can see to that."

"Really? That's not what happened in CMA's last three acquisitions. Employees with seniority were let go to open wiggle room in the overhead structure and then replaced with kids right out of school. The experience mine have is invaluable to patient care and Sandhills has made reasonable contractual commitments to them just as they have to me."

"We generally have not made formal contractual arrangements with individual staff members other than standard job descriptions. We have found at that level they all are about the same."

"Well, you found wrong."

"But in terms of overhead . . . ."

"Look, pal, I don't worry too much about money. I just go by a loyalty list. I paid them the best I could; somewhere around the seventy-fifth percentile of what they could make at the hospital. They knew it was the best I could do."

"This is part of why you were a twenty-fifth percentile earner."

"Maybe so, but I made the ninety-fourth on Boards."

Harper didn't comment.

Lou brought their food. "Bones; your usual. Bacon Swiss CB, Lou's jumbo tater wedges, extra ketchup—'taters and 'maters we call it—and a large vanilla shake topped with caramel and whipped cream. Harper, you get the same, but it's only 'cause of Bones. I was gonna give you the leftover breakfast hash, but he insisted on equal."

Harper didn't acknowledge him.

Bones slid Lou a twenty. "Thanks, pal. Keep the change."

Harper looked at the plates for a moment. Bones traded plates with Harper. "See, you don't even need a food canary here, Riley."

"A food canary?"

"You know, like the miners. They send a canary down into the mines first. If the bird doesn't fly back it's curtains down there." Bones gave a cut-throat sign to emphasize. "When you're in a strange place a food canary might save your a— Uh, I gave up cussing for Mama. Anyway, if the bird goes belly up or beak down you gotta watch out. It's the old 'birdie perched upside down in the cage' trick. I think I learned it from watching 'Get Smart' as a kid." Bones ate one of Harper's tater wedges and then one of his own to demonstrate. "Watch out for seizures, but there won't be any. Lou's clean."

Harper was not amused. "I have been authorized to do what it takes. New car, expense account; hell, boy I'm talking about a million-dollar signing bonus here."

"And my people?"

"Good God, I'm talking more money than you could see in a life-time in that rinky-dink business you own. My bet is it is more than twice what Sandhills is prepared to pay for the entire practice."

"I gotta admit, Mr. Harper, you are a man with a nose for money." Bones laughed. "What's the urgency here? We've known the acquisition was in the works for almost two years. Why are you so worked up now all of a sudden?"

"Hell, don't you realize what's at stake here?" Harper threw a pile of graphs and charts on the table. "Look at this."

"So what am I looking at? What the heck is all this?"

"This is a projected zip code migration pattern study commissioned by my boss, recently completed by Sun Health Consultants out of Atlanta."

"Zip code migration?" Bones asked.

"Yes. A potential loss of millions of dollars; mostly heart cases."

"You know where you messed up, Riley?"

"No."

"Those ain't zip codes, those are people; my people. And yes, I am certain over time some of them will migrate to Sandhills just because of our association with them. It's only natural. I'm sure the study is accurate. I don't know how much your boss paid for that study but it's what I tried to tell you for free when we started this gig. Can't be a prophet in your hometown, I reckon. What you gotta understand, dude, is those aren't numbers. Every one of those zip codes got their chest cracked open to pay for your Porsche car and those marble floors in executive Tower Four where you live. And by the way, tell your surgeons they are quite good. I have no problem with them at all. They sure are gonna be pissed at you if volume falls off next year."

"The hell with all that Pollyanna crap; you gonna sign or not?" Riley was all but screaming now.

"Riley, Sandhills negotiated in good faith the whole way. I can't turn my back on them now. They are number five on my loyalty list already. Until they are disloyal to me there is no going back."

"Damn it, what the hell is wrong with you?"

"I dunno. I guess it's like in 'Cool Runnings.' What's wrong with me? 'Whatever is wrong with you is no little thing.'" Bones laughed.

"You are one more stubborn SOB."

"You're right. I am. But I have prayed God will help me temper it and let me call it tenacity. He's working on me, too. We all have our faults. I promise I'll try to do better."

Harper stood up and began to yell. "Damn it, Robertson you are causing me a lot of trouble. You need to know I know how to get even."

Minnie the Myna squawked a huge wolf whistle and then a short rendition of "Take Me Out To The Ballgame." Lou and Snookers flung open the door and walked in. Bull Wilson stood just behind them, arms crossed like a stoic Kawlijah. The veins popped out on his tree trunk neck and his dark eyes fixed their gaze on Riley Harper.

Bones shook Snook's hand. "Good to see ya, brother." Bones walked up to Bull, hugged him, then tickled the back of his neck the way Bull's grandfather Blinky used to do. "Good to see you too, pal. Whatcha up to these days?"

"Still working for Simmons Rupert and playing semi-pro ball for Durham."

"Cool. Yeah, your granddaddy was a player. You still catching for 'em?"

"Yes, sir."

Harper stood up. "Good God, what is this, some kinda family reunion?"

"Yeah, sorta is, I reckon," Bones said.

Bull walked over and gently pushed down on Harper's shoulder. "You sit."

Harper complied.

"It's okay, guys," Bones said.

"Hell, no, it's not," Snook replied.

Lou spoke up. "Let me explain, Harper. Doc here, he ain't got an aggressive bone in him but he don't got no give up, either. Your best bet is leave him alone. You see, we know what happened to Simon Crutchfield and Bones here knows people who know all that DNA crap. Hell, one of his old classmates is at work on the human genome project. Bluegrass people read, you know. You do understand that DNA business, don't you?"

Harper sat silent.

Lou went on. "There ain't no statute of limitations on the Crutchfield case and old Bones is just a step away from cracking it. And the entire Bluegrass Nation has a copy filed in every lock box and safe around the county. Hell, even Martin Taylor has the file on it. 'Course, it'd take digging up bones to prove it but Bones has been known to do it when indicated, and might just do it, too, if we get provoked."

Harper stood up. "I must be on my way."

Snook and Lou glared at him.

Snook grabbed Riley Harper's arm. "Don't ever set foot in Harvey County again. Go take a long walk by Simon Crutchfield's grave."

"I must go."

Yes, you must." Lou and Snook answered in unison. "Don't let the door hit you on your way out," Lou said.

As he got out of his chair, Bones had one last question. "Mr. Harper. You're right about one thing. That is a lot of money for a country doctor. I gotta ask ya, man, just where is that Pete Stark friend of yours now?"

Harper had no comment. He walked out the door, went to get in his car and scratched out of the parking lot.

They never saw him again.

Harper was relieved of his duties at CMA within three months. The circumstances of his departure were never disclosed. His whereabouts remained unknown for years until one day a small obituary caught Bones' eye.

Chapter Forty One

The signing ceremony was held at Sandhills University at a long mahogany table in the sitting room at the Robertson Library. It might as well have been on the deck of the *Missouri*. All the docs were there, as well as all the VPs from Sandhills. There were a few scattered reporters and a photographer. They took some notes and a few pics, but seemed more interested in the food and light drinks.

Sandhills elected Bones for the keeper of one of the ceremonial pens and Harvey Family chose Sandhills' CEO, Mr. Chevalier, for the other. In the whole process he had been about as visible as the name of the famous band The Seldom Scene, but everyone knew he was the man who set the tone for the negotiations for the big biz crowd. *Fair treatment of primary care docs,* Bones thought. *What a novel concept.*

Bones offered a toast. "Here's to a permanent Medical Home at Sandhills U. We build our foundation on primary care and on that solid ground we stand. We will not fail."

Someone yelled out, "You can't play chess if you ain't got any pawns." Bones laughed so hard he spilled his Co-Cola.

Afterward Bones and Dee broke out the instruments and Billy got out his banjo. He opened the case. There was an envelope in the pick pocket. "Hey, y'all, it's from Brownie Scott." He opened the envelope and unfolded the note inside.

"Read it!" the crowd yelled.

"Okay. Let's see here. It says: "Congratulations, kid. You now have enough music and banjo in ya to make the bluegrass doctor big time. As you know, the banjo you have on loan is a Gibson RB3; the real deal. Not ostentatious, nothing fancy, utilitarian, but a professional-quality instrument; perfect for a real utilitarian workaday doctor who plays semi-pro bluegrass music on his weekends off. You're gonna be the next, Dr. Bones. In honor of the fact you carried on the tradition, and kept the circle unbroken, we hereby now change the status of this banjo from on-loan to ownership. We trust we have resolved any 'Banjo Acquisition Syndrome' issues for you and your Angie on at least a temporary basis. All best wishes, The Brownie Scott Band, The Darin and Brooke Aldridge Band, Balsam Range, Russell Moore and Third Tyme Out, the Grascals, Cuz Alan Bibey and Grasstowne, The Steep Canyon Rangers and Steve Martin, Compass Records of Nashville, Tennessee, and the entire U.S. Navy Fleet in honor of official retired Bluegrass Navy World-Wide Ambassador in perpetuity, Mr. Wayne Taylor and Appaloosa. May your life be a real song."

Bones turned to Dr. Dee. "Wouldn't Indie be proud?"

One of the reporters yawned and scribbled a note to the photographer. *What the hell was that all about?*

Billy rolled thru a bar or two of "Cripple Creek". "Let's get on home and jam a few."

"I agree," Bones said.

Chapter Forty Two

Grinzler Zelnorm called Bones. "Hey, the Kentucky Derby Kid called."

"Better be sure it was the right one."

"How's that?"

"Oh, it doesn't matter. What'd she say?"

"Said Del McCoury said it's okay to let me know you'd struck a deal. Thought you'd call on me for some advice along the way."

"I would have, but we ran aground alone; I turned it all over to Charles Thombley. I listed you as a reference and gave him full permission to ask you anything on our behalf."

"Oh, if you had him you didn't need me. Matter of fact, he touched base with me a couple times in the process. He had a good feel for the local culture for a cat from Atlanta. I'm glad you had him."

"I sure needed someone; I couldn't close the deal alone; no way."

"Are you happy with what you lined up?"

"Yep, it was fair, within Stark guidelines, artistic freedom to practice good medicine without administrative interference; all good."

"Great. Well, this Kentucky girl called and said we needed to play ping pong to celebrate. There's a new Chinese doctor coming to town and they say he's a player."

"Cool. Ping pong. I haven't played in years."

"Neither have I, but we need to play."

"Billy's pretty good. Finished fourth at Wake Forest. Lost to the punter on the football team. The guy went on to punt for the Jets."

"I guess he got a lot of practice punting for Wake."

"Yeah, no first downs for a while there."

"Too much time in the books, I guess. Tough school."

"So why do we need to play so bad?"

"I need to practice up for when the Chinese doc comes to town and we need to go over a few things."

"Okay."

Bones hung up the phone. Interesting. Zelnorm must know something. He had come up in a hyper-competitive market in Mayo, Florida where several institutions battled for turf control. Bones called Mr. Thombley. "I think Grinz wants to talk. You okay with a ping pong game with him?"

"Sure. He understands a lot about the dynamics that will unfold. Just remember, all the details are forever Real Quiet."

"Got it."

As Bones hung up he thought about Grinz. Grinz was a big man, barrel-chested, hairy chest and back, and bald on top. Bones had never known anyone of size who could play much ping pong.

They set up at the Y. Grinz hit a few quick slaps across the table with both speed and precision. Bones caught most of them with a back-hand block but a few got by him. Grinz moved like an agile cat and returned several winners with a loop forehand.

"Hey, man. You can play. Where did you learn?" Bones asked.

"Chinese nanny as a kid in Florida."

"Lord. Chinese soup and ping pong. Good raising, there."

"Yep."

"So whaddaya think about our defection?" Bones asked.

"It isn't a defection. CMA ran you off. They goofed big."

"So what do you think will happen?"

"It's an OBAD deal." Grinzler hit a slam that got by Bones.

"Yeah, I know I'm bad. It's been a long time."

"No, no, not ping pong. The deal."

"Whaddaya mean?"

"OBAD. 'Official Begging Armistice Day.'"

"What's that?"

"It happened that way in Florida. When there was only one institution, then monopoly bred arrogance. I recall one county doc told me about a patient who wanted to see a specialist in a medium-size town. The doc was plenty competent but he was rude and it hurt the patient's feelings. The family doc called this specialist, and said, 'Man, you're a good doc and I trust your medical judgment, but you gotta be nice to people, too. If you hurt their feelings they lose trust and they don't want to come back or send their friends.' The guy said, 'Man, I'm way out here in the Panhandle. No one's gonna replace me.'

"'Gee, I don't know,' the family doc said. 'I always figure there's someone younger and smarter than me who wants my job. The only way I can keep it is at least be loyal to my patients and treat them with dignity.' 'Hell, no one's gonna come here,' he replied."

"So, how did it play out?" Bones asked.

"About five years later Mayo set up a satellite about fifty miles from this specialist's office and he began to lose some referrals to the satellite."

"What did he do?"

Grinz laughed and slapped an over-spin serve right past Bones' forehand. "One day he called the same doctor and asked, 'Hey, are we making your patients happy? I heard some went to the Mayo satellite. Let us know if there's anything we can do for you. Is the staff treating them okay?' Same guy, pre-and post-competition," Grinz said. "OBAD. No one had to beg him for help again, I assure you."

"I bet it's like Indie's old eighty/twenty rule: Eighty percent of people do right because that is their nature. Twenty percent will do right when you understand what motivates them and push the right buttons. Of course, that excludes the sociopaths. You can't do anything with the rapists, pedophiles, chainsaw murderers, et cetera. You just have to hope to not run into them. Grinz, you've always been good to my people so this ain't gonna affect us. I find out what the patient wants and needs and that is what I do. They are my highest priority and always will be."

"That's why you are still in the biz at your age," Grinz said.

"Okay. Let's play best two out of three for a hot dog at the B and B," Bones said.

"You're on."

Chapter Forty Three

Bones dropped by Billy's study near the end of the day the next Wednesday. "Hey, Billy, we're gonna jam at the Bomb Shelter tonight. Moose Dooley's out of town. We need a banjo picker. Can you come?"

"Sure." Billy lay his New England Journal of Medicine on the desk. "You reckon I'm good enough?"

"Of course you are. Besides, we ain't pro pickers. It's not like the doc gig. If we miss a note, no one's gonna die."

"Music does help with the pressure, huh?"

"Yep." Bones twirled his stethoscope in the air. "Brownie Scott's gonna stop in on her way back from their Raleigh gig."

"Dang, man, you just put the pressure back on. I can't play in front of Brownie. She's a pro," Billy grumbled.

"Sure you can. She'll be proud of your progress, I guarantee it."

"You think so?"

"Sure, she's a mama. She told me if her young'un grew up to be just like Billy Spurgeon it'd tickle her to death. You can't ask for a higher compliment from a Southern Mama than that."

"I guess so."

"I know so. She doesn't care how well you play; all she asks is that you play honest. Be true to yourself and do the best you can."

They finished up the office at 5:00, went home to get Kate and Angie, and got to the Bomb Shelter by dark-thirty. Jack had a big bonfire in a fifty-gallon drum just outside the shelter. The flames leapt toward the sky.

"Y'all care for a hot dog?" Jack asked. "We got some left over from the VFW cookout."

"Sure," Bones replied. "We didn't stop to eat today."

Jack smiled. "I don't know how you hold to your nickname, Bones. Never knew ya to miss a meal."

"Adrenaline, I reckon."

Bones and Billy sat by the fire. Kate kissed Bones on the cheek. "We're going on in, hon. Chilly tonight."

"We'll be there in just a minute." Bones finished his hot dog, then lay on his back and peered into the night sky. "Ain't we lucky to live here, Billy? How many doctors in Raleigh get to pick bluegrass at the Bomb Shelter like we do?"

"Very few, Doc, I'm sure."

Bones watched as the flames flickered. "Look at those little embers as they go out in the dark. It reminds me of the fireflies as a kid. We'd catch 'em in a Mason jar, then poke holes in the metal lid with an ice pick so they could get some air. Was like a little lantern. There ain't nothing easier than being a kid. All you have to worry about is getting home in time to see what Mama has cooked up for supper. It's easy to be a kid, and it's easy to be an old man, too. Now a young adult like you, that's hard times. Too many uncertainties; too many decisions. Too hard to figure out who's for you and who's against you. Too much debt, too. Anyway, when we'd get home for supper, we'd let the fireflies go free. Didn't want to kill off anyone who wuz helping us."

Billy laughed. "You know, Doc, there ain't never been a doc who did more for that hospital than you. They did what they could to kill you off. It's strange. I don't understand."

Bones laughed. "I'm glad you don't, Billy. It's a good sign you're a fine young'un and one who will carry on the tradition. I'm proud of you."

Billy turned quiet for a moment. "Hey, Doc, let me ask you something. Word on the street is the hospital tried to sell me down the river, and would have padded your pocket to make it happen. Is that true?"

"Now, Billy, dumb as they were even they know better than to test me on such a thing. Why, you're 'bout like my own young'un. Everyone knows that. I've got my faults, but disloyalty ain't one of 'em. Indie taught me better."

Bones nodded off to sleep. Billy shook him to wake him up. "Hey, Bones! Reveille! Hear that? 'Bugle Call Rag.' That can't be anyone but Brownie Scott. There ain't a man alive who can play it better. Time to go pick."

Bones groaned and began to get up. Billy reached over and extended a hand. "You're getting older, Doc. I owe it to ya to see you through."

"Thanks, Billy boy."

"Let me help you." Billy pulled Bones to his feet.

"I knew I could count on ya. Never had any doubt," Bones said. "Hey, let's put in a request for Brownie to play 'Don't Tread on Me.'"

"Who you gonna dedicate it to, Doc?"

"I dunno, Billy. Your choice."

Billy laughed. "The usual suspects?"

"That'll do." Bones replied.

They went inside to play.

ABOUT THE AUTHOR

Dr. Tommy Bibey grew up making house calls with his country doctor father. He later attended Lake Forest University and Sandhills Medical School where he picked up first the guitar and then the mandolin. He returned to Harvey County and opened a small clinic as a country doctor. Many evenings he could be heard playing the mandolin for patients in his office or if necessary the Hospital. More than one patient has asked him to play at their funeral.

He always viewed medicine and bluegrass music as the two healing arts of the body and soul. Over the years he became stressed when he saw the medical profession move into the need for profit and away from a focus on healing. Every morning he started to play his mandolin, then write stories to relieve the stress. Soon a novel was born then another.

"Acquisition Syndrome" tells the story of what happens when a simple country doctor is squeezed by outside forces to put profit before patients. It is a follow up of *"The Mandolin Case"* released in 2010 which was about how greed blinds some

Feel free to contact him on FaceBook.

Printed in Dunstable, United Kingdom

85047110R00139